Harriott Wight Sherratt

Mexican Vistas Seen from Highways and By-Ways of Travel

Harriott Wight Sherratt

Mexican Vistas Seen from Highways and By-Ways of Travel

ISBN/EAN: 9783337210748

Printed in Europe, USA, Canada, Australia, Japan

Cover: Foto ©Andreas Hilbeck / pixelio.de

More available books at **www.hansebooks.com**

MEXICAN VISTAS

SEEN FROM

HIGHWAYS AND BYWAYS OF TRAVEL

BY

HARRIOTT WIGHT SHERRATT.

CHICAGO AND NEW YORK

MDCCCXCIX

" And they journeyed from Mount Hor by the way of the Red Sea to compass the land of Edom; and the soul of the people was sore discouraged because of the way."

TO THE DEAR COMPANION OF ALL MY TRAVELS,

MY HUSBAND,

THIS VOLUME IS AFFECTIONATELY

INSCRIBED.

CONTENTS.

CHAPTER I.
Preparations for Departure. Vaccination. Study of Spanish. Some Necessities. Money. Shopping. Drinks. Baths. Food. Fruits. Mexican Houses. Hotels. Chambermen. Railroads. Street Cars. Charms of Mexican Travel. 23

CHAPTER II.
Historical. The Toltecs the First Republicans. The Chichemecs. The Aztecs. The Spanish Rule. The Struggle for Independence. Iturbide. War with the United States. Juarez' Government. The Passing of the Brigands. The Church. The Different Races in Mexico. 37

CHAPTER III.
Over the Border. The Custom House. The Central Plateau. Torreon. Zacetecas. The Fountain in the Plaza. The New Woman. The Markets. The Street Cleaners.* Mexican Penal System. Police. The Cathedral. The Plaza at Night. Guadalupe. The Cathedral and Industrial School. A Mexican Apothecary. 44

CHAPTER IV.
An Interpreter and a Mexican Doctor. 54

CHAPTER V.
A Mexican Watering Place. The Baths. The Cathedral and Plaza of San Marcos. A Mexican Schoolboy. The Municipal School. An American Home in Mexico. Drawn-Work. . . . 61

CHAPTER VI.
Some Uncomfortable Neighbors. Marfil. A Great Mining Town. The Opera House. The Methodist Medical Mission. The Pantheon. The Prison. Hidalgo the Hero. Homes of Guanajuato. In the Plaza. 66

CHAPTER VII.
Querétaro. A Night Adventure. A Plaza Breakfast. Maximilian. The Hill of the Bells. The Museum. Querétaro Opals. Hercules Cotton Mills. The Aqueduct. 75

CHAPTER VIII.
Nochistongo Canal. First View of Mexico. Search for a Hotel. Street Cars. Cabs. Destruction of the Maine. Shopping in the Capital. Mexican Herald. Humane Society. Amateur Bull Fights. The Senorita Bull Fighters. Orrin's Circus. The Theaters. 81

CHAPTER IX.
Mexico in Cortés' Day. The Flight of the Spaniards. The Alameda. Alvarado's Leap. The Church of the Martyrs. Pantheon and Campo Santo. The Tree of Noche Triste. The Modern Mexican. Black Eyes. An Adventure. 90

CHAPTER X.
The Cathedral of Mexico. The Zocalo. Academy of San Carlos. A High-Priced Guide. National Museum. National Palace. Monte de Piedad. 99

CHAPTER XI.
The Church Parade. Physique of the Mexicans. A Mexican Mob. Sunday Afternoon on the Paseo. The Paseo. Public Monuments. Chapultepec. The Mexican Cadets. The Palace. Unpopular Americans. The Señora's Opinion. The Wife of the President. The Republic. Diaz. . . . 106

CHAPTER XII.

The Floating Gardens. La Viga Canal. The So-Called Fruit of Romanism. Santa Anita. The Village of Mexicalcingo. Cortés' Bridge. Ixtapalapan. Hill of the Star. Rekindling of the Sacred Fire. 118

CHAPTER XIII.

A Wooden Saint—Our Lady of Los Remedios. The Saint in Politics. The Cloth Saint—Our Lady of Guadalupe. Guadalupe, the Holy City, its Sacred Spring and Chapels. The Stone Sails. The Cathedral and Tilma. 125

CHAPTER XIV.

Interesting Towns in the Vicinity of Mexico. Popotla. Tacuba. Atzcapotzalco. An Overworked Ghost. The Ancient City of Tlanepantla. Jail Delivery of Merchandise. Tacubaya. Mixcoac. San Angel. Coyacan. Battlefields of Cherubusco, Casa Mata and Molino del Rey. Tlalpam. Texcoco. A Stern Sovereign and a Poetic and Indiscreet Prince. The Coalition. 135

CHAPTER XV.

Cuernavaca. A Beautiful Climate. Gardens of La Borda. Palace of Cortés. The Market Place. Donna Juana. On the Housetop. 146

CHAPTER XVI.

The Morning Train. The Mexican Railroad, or "Queen's Own." Duties and Pleasures of the Mexican Women. A Mexican Commercial Traveler and Apizaco Canes. In the Cañon of the Maltrata. Cañon of the Infernillo. Orizaba. The Cotton Factory. The Sugar and Coffee of Orizaba. The Four Cascades. The Bebehañas. 154

CHAPTER XVII.

Cañon of the Metlac. Cordova. Vera Cruz and Its Birds of Prey. Cortés in Vera Cruz. The International Railroad. Jalapa. The Public Lotteries. Coatepec. Some Mexican Bridal Couples. . . 163

CHAPTER XVIII.

Mexican Human Owls. An Early Breakfast. A Trip Over the Mountains. Perote. Mexican Haciendas. Malintzi. The Holy City of Puebla, Its Salads and Its Battlefields. Puebla Onyx. The Cathedral. Holy Week. A New Saint. A Search for a Bath. Another Holy City—Cholulu. Pyramid of Cholulu. Quetzalcoatl. The Sunday Markets. The Churches. The Bull Fights and the Beggars. 172

CHAPTER XIX.

On the Road to Oaxaca. Oaxaca. The Ruined Cities. The Indian Idols. Cathedral and Church of San Dominguez. The Southern Cross. Diaz and Juarez, the Sons of Oaxaca. 190

CHAPTER XX.

The Start for Mitla. The Zapotec Indians. The Big Tree of Tule. The Wayside School. The Organ Pipe Cactus. Tlacolulu. The Hacienda at Mitla. The Indian Village. The Ruins. The Temple Dwelling. The Teocalli. The Custodian. Evening in the Court. 198

CHAPTER XXI.

Impressions of a Traveler. Americans in Mexico. Thrifty Paupers. A "General Promoter of Industries." Estimate of the Northern Indian. Mexican Lack of Mechanical Ingenuity. The Law in Regard to the Switchmen. Lack of Business Principles Among the Mexicans. From Puebla

to the City of Mexico. Tlaxcala. Hacienda of
a Mexican President. Return to the Capital. . 209

CHAPTER XXII.

A Mountain Adventure.˙ San Marcos. Some Agreeable Traveling Companions. At the Fonda. A Slave Woman. An Indian Meal. In Strange Company. Over the Mountains in a Chariot. The Indian Chairmen and Their Dogs. The Indian Mountain Villages. The End of the Journey. The Head-Man and the Village Schoolmaster. An Unconquered Race. The Homes, the Customs and the Dress of the Mountain Aztecs. . 216

CHAPTER XXIII.

Sunday at the Mountain Mission. A Mission School. A Projected Industrial School. An American Baby's Mexican Christening. An Aztec Schoolmaster and His Pupils. The Descent of the Mountains. Other Traveling Companions. . 230

CHAPTER XXIV.

From Mexico to Toluca in the Trail of the Brigands. Toluca. A Midnight Departure. Protection of Human Life in Mexico. Engaging a Sleeper. Acámbaro. Lake Cuitséo. Living Statuary in Bronze. Morelia. Osguerra Hotel. The Zocalo and the Cathedral. The Calzada, the Aqueduct and the Parks. An Invitation to Microbes. Plaza of the Martyrs. Some of the Martyrs. Public Institutions and Advantages of Morelia. . 240

CHAPTER XXV.

The "Lake Country" of Mexico. Lake Patzcuaro. An Abandoned Journey. Patzcuaro. A Trip by Freight Train. Room No. 9. 250

CHAPTER XXVI.

In Celaya. Dirt, Dulces and Opals. Irapuato. An American Hotel. Mexican Nighthawks. On the Road to Guadalajara. Guadalajara. Its Beautiful Women. Religion and Politics. The Assumption of the Virgin. The Markets. The Barranca. The Hospicio. The Park Concerts. San Pedro. Falls of San Juanacatlan. Some Pigeon-Toed Warriors. A Composite Company. Mexican Summer Resort. 256

CHAPTER XXVII.

The Strawberries of Irapuato. San Miguel de Allende. A Pig-Loving Saint and His Wax Colleague. The Home and the Neighborhood of Hidalgo. San Luis Potosi. A Beef Menu. The Excursionists. On the Road to Tampico. Tamasopa Cañon in a Fog. Rascon. El Salto del Abra. Choy's Cave. Las Palmas. The Strange Disappearance of No. 4. Tampico. Some Homesick Americans. Price of Foods. . . 266

CHAPTER XXVIII.

Turning Northward. The Battlefield of Buena Vista. Angels of Buena Vista. Saltillo. Monterey. An American City. Saddle Mountain. The Belt Line Horse Cars. The Bishop's Palace. Capture of Monterey. The Bridge of La Purisima. Topo Chico Hot Springs. Hidalgo Park. A Mexican Festival. 274

CHAPTER XXIX.

Across the Border Again. An Inquisitive Custom House Official. The Custom House Face. A Grumpy Pullman Car Conductor. American Hats and Garments. The Wooden Houses of the United States. 282

ILLUSTRATIONS.

	Page.
Senora Diaz	Frontispiece.
Home of an Aristocrat	30
A Wayside Shrine	35
Maguey Field	39
Home of a Peon	41
Woman Making Tortillas	43
Plaza and Fountain, Zacetecas	55
Excursionists Buying Drawn-Work	65
Hidalgo	71
Corner of the Plaza, Guanajuato	73
Hill of the Bells	78
A Street in the Capital	84
Great Spring Near Hercules	87
Cathedral of Mexico	103
Aztec Woman With Distaff	105
Hill and Castle of Chapultepec	110
President Diaz	115
The Viga Canal	119
Cortés' Bridge	121
Holy Stairway, Guadalupe	131
Stone Sails	134
Trail in the Barrancas	135
Cortés' Palace, Coyacan	140
Gardens of La Borda, Cuernavaca	144
Lake in Gardens of La Borda	148
Market Place, Cuernavaca	151

ILLUSTRATIONS

In a Coffee Grove, Orizaba	155
Pyramid of Cholulu	167
A Mexican Hacienda	173
Hotel Corridor, Puebla	176
Aguadors, City of Mexico	183
On the Streets of Cholulu	186
A Zapetec Woman	191
President Benito Juarez	195
Ferry at Puente Real	196
On the Road to Mitla	199
An Organa Hedge	201
A Crumbling Wall	204
Specimens of Mosaic	207
The Burden-Bearers	214
An Aztec School	218
Across the Mountains	223
Descent Into the Valley	226
Aztec Loom—Four Generations	228
Morelos	231
The Mission Church	234
The "Decent Fonda"	237
A Mountain Home	241
The Aqueduct, Morelia	244
The Calzada, Morelia	246
Plaza de Armas and Cathedral, Guadalajara	248
Hacienda at Lake Patzcuaro	252
Falls of San Juanacatlan	263
Up Tamasopa Cañon	264
Mexican Nat. R. R. Station, San Luis Potosi	267
Bishop's Palace, Monterey	276
Hidalgo Park, Monterey	280

INTRODUCTION.

In this chronicle—which I hope is not altogether gratuitous—of our travels and adventures in Mexico I have endeavored to answer some of those questions which present themselves to the tourist upon the eve of departure for that country. Such queries often remain unanswered, for, as our neighbor republic is constantly changing, the guide-books speedily become ancient history, while the really artistic folders furnished by the railways and the tourist agencies treat only of their own particular routes and consequently give but slight glimpses of the landscape and the people. While aiming to supply this lack I have also in these pages, which are transcribed almost literally from my notebook, endeavored to bring our neighbor over the way a little nearer to us, hoping that we may some day know her better and learn to feel for her the interest of a sympathizing elder sister.

To know our neighbor it will be necessary to visit her, and she is well worthy a visit. It is true that she is given over to germs so that we were almost forced to believe that the Mexicans belonged to the great Germanic race; nevertheless the cities of Mexico are not so offensive as Constantinople or even some of the cities of southern France and Italy, while her balmy air, her magnificent ruins and her prehistoric architecture compensate, in some degree, for her lack of pictorial art. It is also true that we missed the Pullman cars and the many creature comforts of our latter-day civilization, but it is a wholesome experience for the twentieth century American to revert again for a season to the simple ways of his fathers.

In the future our country will doubtless be brought into closer and closer relations with the Spanish-American nations of this continent. The only way we can deal justly with them is to endeavor to see things as far as possible from their point of view. Although this point of view may often seem to us childish and puerile, we may, nevertheless, while leading our neighbors up the steep grade of civilization, also chance to learn something of them. We might even take a lesson in that graceful idleness which would be such a relaxation to the strain of our busy lives, for if we do not speedily mend our ways it is not an utter impossibility that long after the Anglo-Saxon race on this continent shall have died out from overwork and nervous exhaustion the Latins of Mexico may languidly roll their cigarettes under the shadow of the trees and sleepily speculate upon the causes of our downfall.

But let us dismiss these unwelcome imaginings and come back to the present which is still our own. Do you, my tourist friend, take with you on your journey to Mexico a happy philosophy for hardships and a disposition to see in her people neither spectacles nor beggars, but kindly neighbors? Live as nearly as possible an Aztec idyl with the idle Aztecs and make little use of your nose. Study your Prescott on the spot and know the romance of the land and the people and realize if you can that this toiling multitude is the same proud race that defied Cortés, that threw off the Spanish yoke, that put the army of the United States upon its mettle, that repelled the French invasion. From its humble ranks has risen many an apostle of freedom, many a hero.

And what does it matter if the modern Mexican be a little careless of his dates and his figures —what if he does forget his appointments to-day? For him a to-morrow is coming as full of sunshine and soft airs as the present, and after that another to-morrow, and another and so on, indefinitely; so why should he distress himself that the duty of the moment is unfulfilled? Has he not good sense on his side? In our neighbor's opinion all desirable things are hidden in the mañana, therefore let us hope that in the mañanas to come Mexico may find a glorious future for her government and her people.   H. W. S.

Rockford, November, 1899.

MEXICAN VISTAS.

CHAPTER I.

When we—Ahasuerus and I—made ready for a winter in Mexico, we neglected one important precaution—we were not vaccinated; a mistake which, later, caused me much anguish of spirit. Many a night, as I tossed sleeplessly on my hard pallet while the wicked flea pursued me, I imagined myself in the first stages of the smallpox. I arranged my worldly affairs, disposed of my humble belongings, and in my mind's eye saw myself going home as fast freight. My first bit of advice, then, to the traveler intending to visit Mexico is—be vaccinated.

While temporarily disabled by vaccination it is a wise thing to study Spanish—not the Spanish of Cervantes or of Calderon—but those minor classics as presented by the Meisterschaft or any good Natural Method Primer, for it is very convenient, even if you cannot discuss abstruse subjects in the

Castilian tongue, to be able to check your baggage, order your meals, buy tickets, read the posters, and be ready with the usual forms of courtesy.

There is a difference of opinion as to the best time to visit Mexico. We went in the winter. The Mexicans assured us that we made a mistake. If we had gone in the summer, we should, without doubt, have also made a mistake. But whether in the winter or in the summer, it is well to go by one route and return by another. The ideal way for those who love sea travel is to enter Mexico by land and leave it by water. In such case, however, it is prudent to make some previous arrangement with the War Department, for a certain tourist who could not endure the long overland journey was compelled to wait in Mexico all last summer for the cessation of hostilities between the United States and Spain.

Of course it is well to carry with you a camera; but use it, except for natural scenery, as little as possible, for the Mexicans, who are both proud and sensitive, object to being photographed. It is sometimes possible for a few centavos to obtain a sitting from the children or even from a peon, but it is courteous as well as politic to defer to the prejudices of the people. Above all, do not forget your smoked glasses, and if you have plenty of trunk room it is wise to take a pillow, for the Mexican pillows, both in form and substance, are like bricks.

The value of the Mexican coins is soon learned. The centavo—a copper coin—is the Mexican cent; the media is six and one-half centavos; the real, twelve and one-half centavos; dos real, twenty-five, and cuatro real, fifty centavos. The big silver peso, or Mexican dollar, is worth—according to the market value of silver—anywhere from forty-two to forty-seven cents of our money. The traveler in Mexico has ample opportunity to study the advantages and disadvantages of the Bryan creed. When he crosses the border he will be for once in his life rich. His dollars will be doubled, and the wear of his pockets as well.

One peculiar thing in Mexico is the fact that each town has practically the monopoly of its special line of goods. You will be sorry if you do not buy drawn-work in Aguas Calientes and opals in Querétaro. The dulces of Celaya, which taste like condensed milk, are better in their native place than elsewhere. Leon is the saddle town, but while acknowledging the superior beauty of Leon saddles I must insist that the carved leather belts, card cases, and bags made in Mexico are inferior to those made in California, which are almost as cheap, are certainly less clumsy, and, most important of all, have no odor, and consequently do not require antiseptic treatment. Of course the shops in the City of Mexico handle, to some extent, all Mexican goods, but the prices are higher and the assortment less varied than in the towns where they form a staple.

The question what shall we eat and wherewithal shall we be clothed in Mexico is easily answered. By all means wear your most disreputable garments and eat what is set before you, giving thanks that it is no worse. But the question of drink is an ever-recurring problem. The American constitution, unlike that of the Latin races, requires water. This weakness, in a land where the water supply and the sewage have a way of getting mixed, and where all the springs and fountains are used as public laundries, is, to say the least, unfortunate. The natives drink pulque made from the century plant, and great fields of this plant—a species of agave—cover the country. Indeed, a Mexican pulque plantation is more valuable than an American distillery or brewery, and, perhaps, does more harm than either. The blossom stalk of the plant, just before blooming, is cut down, and the sap that flows from it is gathered by men and boys, who insert a gourd into the cup-like cavity at the base of the stem, and placing their lips to one end of it draw the liquid into the gourd by suction. The gourd is then emptied into a sheep or pig skin which imparts a rich flavor to the sap. After one day's fermentation the liquid becomes pulque—a sweet, stringy, nauseous drink. The second day, however, it tastes like koumiss, and is quite appetizing; but in either stage, if enough is taken, it produces an intoxication similar to that of morphine. Nevertheless the wise ones say that pulque should be used by the traveler, both on account of its anti-bilious qualities, which adapt it specially to the climate, and as a specific for kidney trouble. The milky draught did not tempt us, however, so we drank Apollinaris and siphon water (which we suspected were manufactured and charged at the nearest fountain), sour Spanish wine and yeasty beer, All the time in the dry air of the high altitudes, we perished of thirst and dreamed continually of the hydrants and the pure water of home.

Personally I should like the Mexican better if he spent more money on baths and less on cigarettes; but doubtless the Mexican would find me more attractive if I spent less on baths and more on rouge and face powder. It all depends upon one's point of view, and the Mexican has reason to think very poorly of water in any form. We considered ourselves fortunate that, upon our arrival in the Capital, we were able to secure rooms with a bath; but the water had so fetid an odor that while bathing it was necessary to tie a handkerchief over the nose, so we were in the end driven to patronize the baths of Pane y Osorio on the Paseo. This water, which comes from natural springs, is sweet and clear, the tubs are clean, and the service all that could be desired. To an American, whose thoughts are constantly directed to the subjects of pure water and proper sewerage, the apathy of the Spanish-American in this respect is incomprehensible. The great sewerage canal which has been so long in progress will, if ever finished, be a boon to the City of Mexico; for with proper sanitary conditions the Capital will be one of the healthiest cities in the world.

Do not expect a home diet in Mexico. The Mexican bread, which is raised with pulque instead of yeast, is generally sour and sad-colored, while, on account of the lack of refineries in the country, the sugar, though sweet and pure, is very dark and coarse. Tea as served by the natives is a singular brew, and the coffee, which has the rich flavor of furniture polish with an after tang of liniment, is about as bad as can be conceived. At many of the hotels and restaurants the extract of coffee is served with hot goat's milk, and, according to the testimony of the wise ones, this long-suffering animal also furnishes the lamb and mutton chop of the country.

Nevertheless Mexican cooking, when good, like

French cooking, which it much resembles, is delicious. (When I speak of French cooking I mean real French cooking—not that horrible conglomeration of sauces which many Americans call French cooking.) To be sure we did not care for those heavy little pancakes, the tortillas, nor for *chile con carne*—beef with red peppers—but we liked the frijoles, and the soups were perfect. The salads too—of chicory, curly lettuce, creamy alligator pear, tomatoes, and little shreds of onion—are very appetizing. The fruits are sickeningly sweet, which just suits the Mexican, who has a sweet tooth. The granaditas are little pomegranates inclosing a most delicious pulp. The zapotes, which are yellow and green inside, and of a cheesy texture, look on the outside like baked potatoes, resembling in this respect the Cuban sappodilla, albeit they lack the beautiful salmon-pink heart which makes the Cuban fruit so enticing. The mangoes and chiramoyas, although insipid to the stranger, are favorite fruits with the Mexicans, who also delight in the melons, which are really very good, although coarser than ours. We had in the tropics a curious fruit called papaya. It is the melon from which vegetable pepsin is made. It looks tempting and tastes like what it is—a medicine.

At first glance the Mexican house seems very charming and peculiarly adapted to a warm climate;

HOME OF AN ARISTOCRAT, MEXICO.

but the patio, or court, is open to the stars, and the temperature of the table-lands of Mexico does not demand such a sweep of air. Indeed the climate of the plateau is much like that of southern California —perhaps a little milder—and one who has been in California in the winter will realize how uncomfortable is the cold weather in a country which has not a single fireplace or chimney. In fact, although dressed more warmly than at home, we often shivered in our furs. Nor is the patio better adapted to the warm lands near the coasts, especially as the Mexicans use the court for a stable. One sultry morning, as we were passing a beautiful house in one of the cities of the *tierra caliente*—a house which we had often eulogized as the typically elegant Spanish home—a troup of donkeys came plunging through the open door of the court. We looked in and saw the paved patio covered with straw, refuse, and the filth of a barnyard, while the fragrance of all the blooming flowers could not conceal the fact that thirty donkeys had spent the night in the court. Indeed, my susceptible nose too often apprised me of the fact that somewhere behind all the vases and bronze balustrades of the picturesque houses dwelt, in the fullest intimacy of family life, the cattle and the horses. The floor of the patio and of the rooms opening off from it are paved with brick, and as they are seldom swept—especially if cared for by a woman—they are ruinous to gowns and petticoats. The beds are, almost without exception, snowy clean, and the sheets and pillow-cases are starched—not at all a bad idea in a warm climate. Americans usually complain of the hard beds, and we ourselves bore upon our persons impressions of all the different patterns of spring-beds used in the republic. It is a cheap and novel method of tattooing.

The hotels in Mexico, which are upon the European plan, aim to furnish meals more or less palatable, and there are besides, in the vicinity of the inns, good restaurants. When one learns the ways of the cafés one can be very comfortable, and if the sojourner in the hotel does not make the fatal mistake of giving too large a fee to the servants—who are accustomed to receive a few pennies only—he is tolerably sure of good service. In most of the hotels the rooms are cared for by chambermen instead of maids. They are generally neat, careful and obliging. It is better to give the soiled linen to the chamberman, who has usually in his employ some person who will wash it better than it can be done in the eminently unsatisfactory steam laundries. The linen will come back in a sieve-like condition from being rubbed upon the stones, but it will be delightfully clean and fresh.

The railroads of Mexico, like those of Europe, use first, second, and third class cars. Even the first-class cars are, however, none too comfortable, and the third-class are much poorer than the third-class cars abroad. Except on special or excursion trains no Pullman cars are seen south of the City of Mexico. The stage-coaches also sell first and second class fares, but although the accommodations seem about the same for both class passengers, it is better to buy first-class tickets—unless you wish to get out and push when the stage sticks in a slough.

There are no electric roads in Mexico. The street cars are drawn by cheerful little mules which gallop along to the music of tooting horns and cracking whips. The yellow cars are first-class, the green cars second-class. The streets of the cities change their names every block, or if they retain the name, they number—as, San Carlos 1, San Carlos 2. This peculiarity of nomenclature is particularly bewildering to strangers, and one is obliged to watch the trails lest he should be lost.

On the whole, however, in spite of all inconveniences and annoyances, if one is strong, cheerful and a good traveler, I know of no more delightful and profitable trip than a journey through Mexico, especially if one can give time to go into the mountains or into some of the lost corners of the country which are not generally visited by the tourist. Nor need one fear to venture in remote places, for life and property are safer in Mexico than in some parts of our own land. The arm of the law is long and sure, and robbers and murderers are given a short shrift. The trial is held over the remains of the executed criminals, and the jury are apt to bring in a verdict of guilty without leaving their seats. Pickpockets are said to abound in the City of Mexico, but we had no personal experience of them; indeed, except in Vera Cruz, we found the people almost invariably honest, and although we often wearied of dirt and foul smells we liked both Mexico and the Mexicans. They are an extremely courteous people. The raggedest peon lifts his hat in salutation to his shabby comrade, whom he invariably addresses as "Señor." The strain of Indian blood in the nation gives it both gravity and dignity, and through the influence of education our neighbors are fast becoming enlightened. The compulsory education law is strictly enforced, and it is a common thing to see the policeman haling some truant off to school. The schools, which are supported by the government, are in many respects equal to our own.

While I will not deny that the charms of Mexico are greater in the retrospect than in the experience, still there is always for the traveler some interesting and novel spectacle. To stroll along the deceptively clean streets, to chat with the picturesque old women who are selling lottery tickets, to gaze upon the gay cavaliers with their peaked hats, spindle legs, and short-jacketed bodies—whom Palmer Cox must surely have taken for his model of the Brownies—is diversion enough. Then, too, there are long stretches of battlemented or stuccoed walls bearing upon their sun-flecked surfaces the inscription "No Fijar Annuncios" (Post no bills); there are glimpses of flower-decked

A WAYSIDE SHRINE.

courts and dusky Cathedral interiors; and when one is weary, there is always the tiny zocalo or plaza near the Cathedral, and the embowered aisles of the great city parks, where one may sit among the roses, and watch the changing throng. When all these delights pall upon the traveler, he can take long excursions by the mule-cars to quaint, ill-smelling towns, whose half-clothed inhabitants will greet him, Mexican fashion, with outstretched, open hand. To the citizen of the United States, who has no preconceived prejudices, this Spanish-American world is a new and fascinating one.

These neighbors of ours, who speak a different language, think different thoughts, and live different lives from our own, are well worthy our serious consideration, our sympathy, and our friendship.

CHAPTER II.

There is no record of the people who occupied Mexico before the coming of the Toltecs. We know, however, that the Toltecs, a wandering tribe from the north, invaded the country about the year 650, and that at the time the Goths and Lombards were overrunning southern Europe they had already established in Mexico a mighty empire. These newcomers found the city of Tula already a flourishing town. They rebuilt it, gave to it its present name, and made it their capital. Mitla, which was named for the great King Mitl, was one of their sacred cities, and at Teotihaucan, another of their holy places, they built the famous Pyramids of the Sun and the Moon.

From the remains now found in Mexico, it is evident that the Toltecs were a civilized people. They excelled in the arts and sciences of those days, as well as in architecture. Strangely enough these far-away people were the first to introduce the republican form of government into Mexico. The Toltec kings were allowed to reign for fifty-two years, but if a sovereign died before the expiration of that time the law provided that a republic should replace the monarchy for the unexpired term. In acknowledgment of his wise reign Mitl, the good king, had his official life prolonged seven years, and after his death his widow was allowed to fill out the unexpired term. She was succeeded by her son, a dissolute prince, under whose sway the Toltec supremacy rapidly declined. Internal dissensions contributed to sap the life of the nation, and before William the Conqueror fought the battle of Hastings, the Toltecs were scattered. More than half a century later Mexico was again invaded by a northern horde, the Chichemecs, a tribe of barbarous hunters, dressed in the skins of wild beasts and living in caves. The Chichemecs in time gave way to the Aztecs, who also came from the north, and sweeping down upon the great central plateau, conquered the country.

The Aztecs founded a powerful empire, which lasted two hundred years, or until the coming of the Spaniards. This empire Cortés destroyed, and governed the conquered nation in the name of Spain. After his death, the government was administered by a succession of Spanish viceroys, sixty-four in number. The last of these viceroys bore the extremely un-Spanish name of John O'Donahue, spelt in Spanish, Juan O'Donaju.

MAGUEY FIELD—*page 26.*

In the year 1810 Hidalgo, a parish priest, inaugurated a rebellion against Spain. The following year Hidalgo and his three generals were captured and executed; but the cause for which these brave men died did not die with them, and the struggle continued until 1821, when Spain acknowledged the independence of Mexico.

The first president of the Mexican republic was Augustin Iturbide. Soon after his election a move was made to change the republic into a monarchy, and the crown was offered to a royal prince of Spain. This offered kingdom, which, so far as territory was concerned, was one of the greatest in the world, was refused, and in 1822 Iturbide foolishly allowed himself to be proclaimed emperor. The new emperor and his wife were solemnly crowned in the great Cathedral of Mexico. But Iturbide was soon obliged to flee for his life, and in 1824 he was captured and shot. The other Mexican emperor, Maximilian of Austria, was, in 1867, also executed by the decree of the Mexican republic. Between these two hapless emperors there were more than fifty presidents and dictators, and three hundred revolutions.

As a result of the war with the United States, occasioned by a dispute over a small strip of land between the rivers Nueces and Rio Grande, Mexico was obliged in 1848 to cede half of her immense territory to this country, and the United States afterward bought from her the southern half of Arizona. In spite of this shrinkage in real estate Mexico has still on her hands more land than she, with her present methods, can care for.

After the execution of the Emperor Maximilian at Querétaro, President Benito Juarez, a full-blooded Indian, ruled Mexico wisely and firmly. He died in 1871. In 1876 General Porfirio Diaz headed a successful revolution, and was elected to the presidential chair. Since then Diaz, who is a patriot and a wise ruler, has been many times re-elected president.

President Juarez, upon his election, immediately gave his attention to the enforcement of the laws against brigandism. Upon the principle that "it takes a thief to catch a thief," the shrewdest criminals were, upon conviction, compelled to serve on the police force. This plan, which invested criminals with a sense of responsibility in the government of the country, worked finely. Brigands taken prisoners were compelled to serve against brigands, a scheme which was speedily fatal to the brigandism fostered by long periods of disorder occasioned by the wars. By edict Juarez also freed the government from the power and the exactions of the church. For a time—although Mexico is a Catholic country—no priests were allowed to walk

HOME OF A PEON.

the streets in priestly robes, the ringing of the church bells was regulated by law, and the rich decorations of the churches themselves were confiscated for the good of the republic. Unfortunately, there now seems to be a growing revulsion of popular feeling. The long black mantle worn by the priest too often fails to conceal the vestment beneath, the bells are rapidly becoming once more a nuisance, and the church bids fair to attain its old-time wealth and power. Republican institutions in Mexico have more to fear from this silent, inward force than from any other foe.

The people of Mexico are of three races. The white race, which comprises about twenty per cent of the population, is of Spanish or European extraction. The people of this race generally hold the government offices, and consider themselves the superior class; although social standing, as in Cuba, does not depend upon the race, and a dark skin is no shame in Mexico, where the question of caste is determined, not by color, but by social position, wealth, or culture. Juarez, the most beloved of all the presidents, was a full-blooded Indian, and Diaz himself is a half-breed. The Mexican creoles or mestizos, who comprise nearly one-half of the population, are the descendants of the Spaniard and the Indian. They are the working people of the country—the skilled artisans, the mechanics, the soldiers and the higher servants. As would naturally be expected in a conquered nation, the real owner of the soil, the Indian, or the half-breed in whose veins the Indian blood predominates, is the lowest of all the classes. He is the so-called peon, the man who does the hard work on the haciendas, the toiler, the drudge. The peon, though not really a slave, because of his attachment to the land, often remains for generations on the same estate, and unfortunately this sentiment of loyalty to the sod, combined with the bonds of debt which eternally fetter him, lead to what is practically a life-long enslavement. When the peon drifts into the city he soon becomes a degenerate; and it is unjust to judge the race from the worthless types seen in the large towns. The mountain Indian is a much finer man than the Indian of the plain or the hamlet, although I fear that he has, with the Indian virtues, the Indian imperfections—a lack of ambition and a tendency to drunkenness.

WOMAN MAKING TORTILLAS.

CHAPTER III.

It is strange that so small a stream as the Rio Grande should separate two races, two civilizations, two cycles. From the Anglo-Saxon civilization of to-day we pass, upon crossing the river, to the Spanish-American civilization of one hundred and fifty years ago. As we file out of the train to the custom house we see only dark faces, and sombrero-hatted serape-draped figures, and, most foreign of all, we are treated by the custom-house officials with a gentle courtesy alien to our experience. The examination is soon over—for wine and spirits are the principal dutiable articles—and we dash off into another world—a world whose inhabitants and customs are alike strange to us.

The route by Eagle Pass carries us along the high plateau, in the same path by which the Aztecs entered the country. The plateau, which is from 6,000 to 7,000 feet high, is bordered on both sides by mountain ranges, beyond which the land slips away to the sea. The country is covered with shifting sand, whose only vegetable life is an occasional clump of greasewood or cactus. The distant mountains on both sides of the plateau shut off the clouds that rise from the sea on either hand, and in some of these districts no rain has fallen for seven years, a condition of affairs which by no means adds to the comfort of the traveler.

A ride of fifteen hours brought us to Torreon, where we saw for the first time that curious picture of Mexican life which was afterward to become so familiar to us. The sunny plaza before the station was crowded with peaked-hatted, gay-blanketed Mexicans who, in spite of the heat, wore their serapes twisted closely around them. Their nether man was clothed in the tightest trousers on the thinnest legs I ever dreamed of. With their bulky shoulders and stilt-like legs, these dark-faced dandies, in gay trappings, curiously resembled high-colored birds of the heron family. The women wore bright-hued rebosas, or shawls over the head, and I was interested to see that hoopskirts were still in fashion in Mexico; there were even some old-time tilters in evidence. Both sexes wore great flapping sandals of leather, bound to the foot with thongs of rawhide. No one, however, was naked, as in Cuba.

As the day wore on our surroundings grew more and more picturesque. Mexico is, in fact, more foreign than anything in Europe outside of Turkey.

The quaint figures of the men plowing with oxen and crooked sticks in the fields, the troops of cattle, sheep, and goats, whose red-blanketed herder gives a bright bit of color to the landscape, the little villages where hordes of beggars besiege the traveler with jargon prayers for centavos, all are alike curious and interesting to the tourist who sees the picture for the first time. Nor must we forget that most familiar of all Mexican figures—the woman preparing tortillas for the humble meal. One whom we saw by the wayside was surrounded by a flock of peeping chickens, who took advantage of her interest in the passing train to peck the dough from her hands.

We reached Zacetecas one evening about ten o'clock. For some incomprehensible reason most of the railway stations in Mexico are at a distance from the towns. Zacetecas is no exception to the rule, so we climbed into a dirty old mule-car, and, to the music of a tooting horn, joggled up the hill two miles to the city. As we had more confidence in our command of French than of Spanish, we chose to go to the French hotel. Our landlord, who proved to be a Basque from Bayonne, on the Spanish frontier of France, spoke a thick-tongued dialect, almost incomprehensible, but fortunately he had little difficulty in understanding our peculiar needs. We were ushered into a big, brick-floored room, opening on a balcony overhanging the street. The room, with its two hard pallets, its two dressing tables, two comfortless chairs, and two candles, was a reproduction of a continental bedroom in a village inn. Upon the wall hung two gaudy lithographs— one a picture of the young Mozart playing before the queen and the other a marriage scene interrupted by the appearance of the bridegroom's mistress and child—a decidedly Frenchy work of art.

In the morning, when we looked from our balcony, we saw a long, narrow, cobble-stone paved street winding up a hill; a hill which pilgrims ascend on their knees to the Chapel of Los Remedios. All around Zacetecas the mountains rise like the rim of a bowl. In the bottom and on the sides of the basin lies the town, which like many of the Mexican cities greatly resémbles the crowded hill-towns of Palestine. La Bufa, or the Buffalo Mountain, where Juarez fought one of the battles of the numerous revolutions, overlooks the city. There are gold and silver in all the hills, but neither silver nor gold falls into the hands of the jostling crowds that fill the streets, for—in spite of the fact that they are continually toiling—bitter, crushing, hopeless poverty is their lot. An old man passing one morning under our windows dropped a bag of wheat which broke and scattered the contents in the street. He worked many hours gathering up the precious cereal, grain by grain. Could there be a more touching evidence of patient want than this?

Zacetecas is more than 8,000 feet above the sea, and the rare air of the high altitude renders less apparent the sickening smells that one naturally expects to find in a Mexican city with a swarming population. This is fortunate, for even with the best will for cleanliness, the poorer people of Zacetecas would be obliged to dispense with water, which is scarce and dear in the city. One of the most curious sights in all Mexico is the fountain in the little plaza, where the women gather every morning with their water jars to scoop up the scanty and treasured fluid. With infinite patience these oily tressed Rebeccas scrape up each precious drop, while the "mute, inglorious" Isaacs stand sympathizingly by, and, let us hope, give to their inamoratas, as they stagger off under the weight of the heavy red jars, the aid of their prayers.

I found the "new woman" greatly in evidence in Zacetecas. She didn't know she was a new woman —bless her—but she certainly was one. She fought her own battles, and went into business on her own account, and no man said her nay. I watched with interest the methods of a courageous soul who appeared one morning bearing upon her handsome head a heavy table. She established herself in a sunny spot opposite my balcony, opened an umbrella and a folding chair, took from her bag a small stock of dulces and bananas, and after a spirited contest with the proprietor of the store before which she located, opened shop according to approved methods. A baby slung to her back proclaimed the fact that she had not sacrificed private to public duties, but that her "sphere" included all.

During her business life I saw her sell one banana, and a small boy stole two of her dulces, so fearing that, even in the land of free silver, she would never become a bloated bondholder, I felt myself obliged to give her the support of my humble patronage.

Around the old plaza of the fountain are the markets of the poor people. The ground is thick with venders who sit upon the pavements with their scanty stocks—little piles of potatoes, of peanuts, of oranges, or of onions—spread around them. Here too are sold sausages, chickens, liver, beans or frijoles, chops, garlic, pins, needles, nails, cotton cloth, and the thousand and one necessaries of daily life. The new market, near the grand plaza of the Cathedral, is more pretentious, and is filled with great piles of tropical fruit heaped in tempting mounds.

The streets of Zacetecas are kept clean by the prisoners in the city jail, who are compelled, in chains and under the surveillance of squads of mounted policemen with leveled guns, to work out their fines. From our balcony we watched with sympathy these unwilling workers, but I believe that the system is not, on the whole, a bad one. Indeed, the penal system of Mexico has some advantages over that of our own country. The term of a prisoner in the penitentiary is divided into three periods. The first is given entirely to penal labor; the second allows a little time for amusement, and the third is preparatory for freedom, and the prisoners receive pay for their work and are entitled to various privileges.

The best-dressed and most impressive persons in Zacetecas are the policemen. They wear white caps and neat belted suits of dark blue trimmed across the breast with festoons of white cord. In the day time they carry a baton and swing a revolver from their belts; in the evening they add to their equipment a lighted lantern, and the long rows of these lighted lanterns extending up and down the street at night give the comforting assurance that the guardians of the peace are on duty. These policemen, on the kindergarten principle of keeping mischievous people busy, are often chosen from the most dangerous criminals. I can testify that they are efficient officers, for during one afternoon seven men were arrested under my window. The principal cause of arrest is drunkenness. When the offender cannot pay his fine—and he never can

—he is sent with the chain-gang to work it out.

There is at Zacetecas a very good Cathedral with a wonderfully, but not beautifully, carved front, although for Indian work it is fairly creditable. Inside there is a famous painting, not in the least bad, which is said to have been done by a boy seven years old. While we were in the Cathedral vespers began, and the same boy—or some other one— opened service with the most awful voice I ever heard. Indeed, the music in its entirety was so horrible that it quite thrilled us.

The center of social life in Zacetecas seems to be the plaza near the Cathedral, where the band plays in the evening and the young people promenade. The youths form in line and march in one direction while the maidens march in the opposite one. This is really another market on the plaza, where most of the Mexican marriages are made, for as the two lines pass each other, by some sign known only to lovers an understanding is established, and the maiden is wooed and won. In some of the Mexican cities there is a double ring—one for the upper classes, the other for the lower classes. Our personal advent into the plaza circles of Mexico could hardly be called a social triumph. First Ahasuerus marched with me in the women's procession, and was covered with contumely as with a garment; then I made matters worse by joining his party, and in the end we were only too glad to sit down on a cold stone bench and play the modest part of humble and chilly spectators.

It is an amusing experience to take the street cars in the plaza of the fountain, and slide down by gravity six miles to the town of Guadalupe, where there is a fine old church with a curiously carved front. The church contains a modern chapel overloaded with gilt, said to be the most costly in Mexico. The convent, which was formerly a part of the church, has been confiscated by the government and is used for an industrial school, where boys are seriously and practically taught the different trades. We went into some of the departments and saw the carpenter shop, the serape factory, the hat-braiding and the shoemaking establishments, and the bakery. In this well-ordered institution more than one hundred boys are each year prepared for a life of honest toil.

As I waited in Guadalupe for the coming of the half-dozen panting mules who were to drag us up the steep hills, I seated myself in a drug store and observed Mexican methods of dispensing medicines. The counters of this particular shop were like the rails of a grand altar, and the drugs were stored in carved choir-stalls with glass doors. On the high altar were piled bottles of patent medicines, prominent among them the familiar "bitters" and "tonics" of our own land. The druggist seemed to be a sort of high priest, who prescribed penitential doses and then sold them. Everything was thick with dirt, even to the face and hands of the high priest.

CHAPTER IV.

We were no sooner installed in our quarters in Zacetecas, than a small but important person, clothed in imitation American attire, with a hat all too wide for his shrunk brain, made his appearance. "Señor, Señora," he said. "I am interpreter. I spik the Spanish, I spik also the Inglis. I am at your service. Can I do some tings for you?"

"Yes," I replied. "You can get me some blue glasses. I have broken mine, and this glare blinds me."

The interpreter regarded me for a moment, doubtfully, then he placed his dingy hand on his heart, with a reverent inclination, and said, "Señora, at your service. I go."

He was gone the greater part of the day. When he returned he bore in his arms a number of small packages wrapped in newspaper. He carefully unwrapped the little parcels and placed the contents in a row on the table.

"Señora," he said apologetically, "I find not many

blue glasses; but the Señora may be pleased to like the white glasses; therefore I bring also the white."

I looked at the row of tiny objects, and then walked to the window to conceal a smile. The poor fellow had succeeded in obtaining a quantity of little wine-glasses, some blue, some white. There is not a town in the United States where so curious a collection could have been found. I explained to him, as gently as I could, what I wished, and he rushed away enthusiastically. In a short time he returned with an assortment of goggles that made me shiver, but I selected the most unobtrusive, and wore them as a penance all winter.

The morning after our arrival in Zacetecas I arose, took my usual cold bath, and in a few moments was in the throes of sciatica. I could not move an eyelash without acute anguish. We were in despair, but I put a brave face on the matter, assuring Ahasuerus that I would soon get well by "the light of nature." But the day wore on, and the light of nature seemed to be snuffed out.

"We must have a doctor," said Ahasuerus. "You can't have a fit of sickness in this God-forsaken town."

"I decline to have a serape and sombrero doctor," I retorted despairingly. "He'd give me cactus tea and powdered lizard." However, Ahasuerus was firm, and the landlord was summoned.

"Monsieur," I demanded plaintively, "do you know of a good doctor?"

"Mais, oui Madame," responded the landlord, in his fat-tongued French, "I know a docteur magnifique. He has recovered me when I go to die of the ill in the head."

"All right," exclaimed Ahasuerus, cheerfully. "He's just the fellow I want. What's his address?" he continued, taking out his note-book.

"Comment, Monsieur?"

"Where does this doctor live?"

"In Bayonne, Monsieur. It makes itself near to the border of Spain. He is a great docteur."

Ahasuerus glared wrathfully at the landlord, but the landlord's fat face was impenetrable.

"But do you know no doctor in Zacetecas, Monsieur?" I queried. "I am ill and must have a physician."

"That is great damage," announced the landlord, plaintively. "Madame is ill and takes not the air of Zacetecas."

My private opinion was that Madame had taken too much both of the air and the water of Zacetecas. However, I mildly responded: "Perfectly, Monsieur; you are right. Do you not know a doctor in Zacetecas—a good doctor—who will cure me so that I can get out and see your beautiful city before I leave it?"

"Mais, Si, Madame," with renewed confidence. "I know a docteur very good. He is pharmacien" (druggist).

"A pharmacien? But does he know anything about diseases?"

"Certainement. Madame will tell him that she has a maladie, and then he will know that she is ill, and he will give her an ordonnance" (prescription). "He is bon pharmacien, bon docteur—pour les chevaux" (for the horses).

"A horse doctor?" Ahasuerus and I groaned in concert.

"But, landlord," I protested, "there surely must be some other doctor in town. Can't you tell us of any real doctor?"

"Pardonnez-moi, Madame," replied the landlord, grudgingly, as if at last compelled to reveal a sacred trust. "I know a docteur sage, O, très sage. But he is Germain."

"Very well; I like German doctors; the best doctor I ever had was a German. Does he speak French or English?"

"Madame, the good docteur knows all—all; he is dentista."

"Dentista? But I don't want a dentist; there is nothing the matter with my teeth. I have the rheumatism."

"What is it that I tell you? It is that the good docteur knows all."

"I vote for the dentista," pronounced Ahasuerus, decidedly. "Where can I find him?"

"Monsieur, I send to seek him; Voilà; I haste myself—I run."

Monsieur Jean "hasted himself" with such good results that within the half hour a gentle knock at the door announced the coming of the dentista. Ahasuerus opened the door. An alert, bright-eyed man, in the conventional American dress, appeared, greeted us in perfect English, and in a minute, with quick professional tact, was master of the situation.

"You are in perfect health, except that you suffer," he said. "Why have you the sciatica?"

"I am sure I cannot tell, doctor."

"Did you take a cold bath this morning?"

"Yes; but that didn't hurt me any; I am accustomed to it."

"Nevertheless, that is the cause of the trouble. I have known cold baths to be fatal in Zacetecas. We are more than 8,000 feet above the sea, and evaporation is so rapid that a chill is almost certain to follow a cold bath. The only safe bath here is a hot one, taken at bedtime. The Zacetecans, who know their climate, are said to bathe but twice —once before their first communion, and again after they are dead. Can you take bad-tasting medicine?"

"I can take anything, doctor."

"Good! A model patient. I will send you a Mexican draught that will taste vilely, but I will promise you that you will be well enough to-morrow to walk down to my office and see my new electrical apparatus and the X-ray machine that I have just brought from New York."

The Mexican draught soon arrived in a black junk bottle that had a decidedly disreputable appearance. From the smell and the taste it might have been prescribed by the horse doctor himself. Nevertheless it did its work, and the next day I was able to take the twelve-mile trip to Guadalupe, and to visit the doctor in his cozy bachelor quarters overlooking the Cathedral plaza; and there, in that far-off benighted land, I, a citizen of the United States, and a so-called progressive woman, made my first acquaintance with the X-ray.

As we walked away from the doctor's office—to quote his own words—"no longer patients, but friends"—we spoke sorrowfully of his exile in that far-away land—an exile necessary for climatic reasons, and endured cheerfully and courageously. And we said to each other, "After all, the best missionary is an intelligent and conscientious physician; for surely there is no mission more holy or more Christ-like than the blessed mission of healing."

As we left Zacetecas, Monsieur Jean delivered the following valedictory: "You see; what is it that I tell you? It is that at my house you have all things. You desire the water of minerals—behold the bon Vichy. You wish the glass of blue—it is yours. You demand the good docteur—he is equally at your service. All things you have in my house. Monsieur, Madame, are you content?"

And we were content.

CHAPTER V.

It is well, if possible, to leave Zacetecas by daylight, for, as the train winds up the mountains, there is a charming view of the verdant bowl in which the city lies. The distance to Aguas Calientes is about seventy-five miles, and the scenery along the road, when the dust is not too thick, is thoroughly enjoyable. The Hotel Washington in Aguas Calientes is, Mexican fashion, more than a mile from the station, but the mule-car ride through the quaint, narrow streets is well worth taking.

Aguas Calientes—warm waters—is noted for its baths. The best springs are those near the railway station, where for twenty-five centavos one can have a refreshing bath with the added luxury of a sheet, a towel, a little wash-rag resembling a bird's nest, made of the fiber of the cactus, and a soap tablet. These little tablets make a snowy lather, and are very healing to the skin, and one really wonders why the Mexicans are so wedded to dirt when they have such superior soap. The bathrooms, which are cold cells with stone floors, and stone steps leading down into the tubs set beneath the floor, are not so satisfactory as the baths themselves. The velvety soft water is said to be good for rheumatism, and I believe it, for Ahasuerus and I, after the first trial of it, promptly became confirmed rheumatics.

The Grand Baths, which are about a half-mile east of the station, are open-air baths. They are named for the apostles, and one can take a St. Peter, a St. John or a St. Mark, as best pleases him. They are of different temperatures, but all hot. From the spring at the Grand Baths runs a steaming brook which is used by the poorer people both for laundry and bath-house. The women are always washing on the stones, and sometimes they are sporting in the water. In spite, however, of the glowing romances of the guide-books, we saw nothing fascinatingly improper in these public baths. For studies in the nude, Mexico, as compared to Cuba, offers few advantages. Indeed, we saw nothing in Aguas Calientes that the traveler cannot see at the springs in southern France or Italy.

There is a fine Cathedral at Aguas Calientes and some good churches, all of which contain creditable pictures by a dead and gone local artist—Juan de Lopez by name. In front of the Cathedral is the plaza of San Marcos, which is beautiful—for a tropical park. The parks of the southern lands are never so beautiful as those of our own climate, for dusty orange trees and grassless ·reaches of white sand do not charm the eye as do our great elms and velvety slopes of greensward. In the park we met a Mexican school-boy of sixteen studying his German grammar under the trees. He greeted us with graceful and unaffected cordiality, and seemed to take great delight in our society. He explained that, although Americans came often to Aguas Calientes, and a few were residents of the city, he seldom had an opportunity to speak at length with them. This boy was a pupil in a private school and was studying to be a civil engineer. He told us that the professional men in Mexico are required by the schools to speak English, and that the study of the language is creeping even into' the municipal schools. Our young friend himself spoke English slowly but correctly.

As we came from the park our attention was attracted by a peculiar humming noise. We followed the sound, and found ourselves in one of the municipal or common schools. The Mexican scholars have a way of studying aloud in a half-chant, half-buzz, that is very nerve-racking, and that makes of the school-room a perfect bedlam. In the distance this buzz resembles that of an invading army of grasshoppers.

The Hotel Washington, like many other Mexican hotels, is only one story in height. The long-grated windows of our room encroached upon the sidewalk, so that all the busy life of the streets passed before us, and I could almost touch the little burros as they ambled by. We went one day with a friendly countrywoman to see the house she was fitting up for a home in the city. American ingenuity and American principles of sanitation were making an ideal habitation of the Mexican dwelling. The rooms, of course, all opened on the sunny paved court, and the startling innovations of fireplaces and bathrooms had been introduced. We climbed to the housetop, an important feature of Mexican homes, and we heartily indorsed the schemes of the prudent mistress for strengthening the roof. Certainly the heavy stone roofs of the Spanish-American buildings, which too often rest upon rotted supports of wood, must be a danger to the people. In the kitchen through which we strolled, the range consisted of two little basin-shaped grates for the burning of charcoal, which were inserted in the cooking table.

Of course every one who goes to Aguas Calientes buys drawn-work, which is cheaper and better there than in the City of Mexico. As we were strolling near the depot, one day, an American excursion train came in. In an instant the tourists were besieged by the drawn-work venders, and many a sharp bargain was driven before the train pulled out. It is well for buyers to remember that the work should be done on a good quality of linen, and that the long-thread stitches are neither durable nor desirable.

EXCURSIONISTS BUYING DRAWN-WORK.

CHAPTER VI.

The tourist who is interested in the country through which he passes should make the journey from Aguas Calientes to the City of Mexico by daylight. The sight of the irrigating ditches, the waving wheat fields and the quaint towns along the route will do much to console him for the omnipresent dust. At Leon, whose green valley is a veritable oasis in the surrounding desert, he can buy one of the famous Mexican saddles or an artistic bridle.

We passed a terrible night at Siloa. Our next-door neighbors—Mexicans—talked and laughed at the top of their voices, all night long. When they thought we might possibly be asleep, they pounded upon the walls of the partition and even took the trouble to come out on the gallery upon which all the rooms opened, and knock on our door. The Spanish-American, at least in Mexico and Cuba, is a night-hawk who never sleeps himself, and who resents sleep in others.

At Siloa we left the main line and journeyed through a charming valley as beautiful as that of San Gabriel in California, to Guanajuato. The hillsides were still brown, but when the rains come, and the land bursts into great mounds of bloom and verdure the region must be a paradise. At Marfil, a quaint little village, we took the mule-car for Guanajuato. The line runs up a creek whose bed is full of gold and silver. According to popular report it is the custom in the valley to soak the pigs who wallow in the water, to save the silver deposited in their bristles; but I should not like to be made responsible for that story. We were also told that one-sixth of all the world's supply of silver comes from Guanajuato—another statement I am not prepared to defend with my dying breath. At all events, Guanajuato is a very rich town; not at all like its rival silver town—poor, starving Zacetecas. There is a beautiful opera house opposite the plaza, the finest I ever saw—not even excepting the Grand Opera House in Paris, which may be more costly, and certainly is larger, but not nearly so beautiful. And yet to reach this opera house and the prosperous town, we passed down the cañon of Marfil, three miles in length, and saw the hillsides piled with flat-roofed adobe hovels. Up the steep declivities staggered broken stairways upon which squatted dirty children and half-clothed men and women; while dusty, twisting pathways, which seemed to go down nowhere in particular, sent down clouds of sand upon the passer-by. It was a picture of squalid misery that could hardly be equaled at Zacetecas.

One of our fellow passengers, the only English-speaking person, except ourselves, upon the car, volunteered to show us the way to the Pantheon. When we left the car together he led us, to our surprise, to a pretty vine-embowered Spanish house and introduced us to the Rev. Mr. C. We found we were in the Methodist Medical Mission, the only one of its kind, I believe, in Mexico. Our first acquaintance, Dr. S., had almost completed a hospital of forty beds, for the treatment of the sick of any faith, or no faith—truly a Christ-like enterprise. There is, in connection with the hospital, a church of more than three hundred members, many of them strong men in the community. The work of these missionaries has not been done without opposition. The men who, twenty years ago, organized the movement were twice mobbed, and once escaped with their lives only through the humanity of a "liberal" Mexican, who disguised them as peons and so conducted them through the mob. At present the spirit of hostility to the work of the church is considerably modified.

We made the trip to the Pantheon on burros. I

found burro-riding much more comfortable than the hard mule-riding of which I had had former experience in California. I had no saddle—merely a pack—but the motion was as delightful as that of a rocking-chair. When I came, afterward, to know and to love the Mexican burros, I came to believe in the transmigration of souls, for it seemed to me that the army of saints and martyrs must have gone into the bodies of those patient, kindly, little burden-bearers. Whenever I saw them climbing the cliffs so laden that only their deer-like legs were visible, when I heard the cheery ring of their pretty hoofs upon the stony street, I sent them a blessing from my heart. Surely there is nothing in animal nature, and there is little in human nature, that can excel in faithfulness this patient friend of man.

The Pantheon has a big square wall surrounding a large court. In these walls are the vaults for the reception of the dead, the whole somewhat resembling tiers of postoffice boxes. For the sum of $25 a box may be occupied for five years. At the end of this time the lease may be renewed or a perpetual lease may be obtained. As, however, the perpetual lease costs $125—a fortune even to the well-to-do Mexican—most of the bones are cast out in a few years to make room for others. By the peculiar action of the dry air, the bodies in the vaults become mummified, and if we descend to the underground corridors we shall see long rows of these mummies standing upright, the men on one side of the passage, the women on the other. At the end of the corridor, looking like rubber dolls, are the blackened bodies of the children. We were told the story of a woman who went down into the crypt and was unexpectedly confronted by the body of her husband. Naturally the shock threw her into convulsions. The corridor is about five hundred feet long, and it is two-thirds full of bones which have been taken from the vaults above.

I understand that since we were in Guanajuato, these mummies have, by a decree of the church, been clothed in white linen Mother Hubbard wrappers. This must add to the horrors of the grisly sight, and it seems a wrong to the helpless dead to preserve their bodies in so ghastly a manner. Better is it, a thousand times, to return to the bosom of dear mother earth, and through her marvelous processes of resurrection spring up again in the blooming flowers and the waving boughs.

At the prison in Guanajuato, Hidalgo, the parish priest, struck the first effective blow for Mexican independence. Hidalgo was more than a parish priest—he was philosopher, scientist, and political economist. In his desire to increase the resources of his native land, he planted a vineyard, raised silkworms, and established a porcelain factory. The

D. MIGUEL HIDALGO Y CORTILLA—*page 71.*

Spanish government, jealous of the development of Mexican products, destroyed his vineyard and burned his factory. Hidalgo revolted, and with an Indian army marched upon Guanajuato. The first attack was made from the mountain overlooking the prison, but the stones and paltry firearms of the Indians proving of little avail against the thick walls of the fortress, one of the insurgents volunteered to carry, after the manner of his people, a flag-stone upon his back, and under the protection of his burden, fire the fortress doors. The plan succeeded, the humble hero burned the doors, and Hidalgo's band entered and slew the Spaniards, whose blood still stains the wall and stairway. A year later Hidalgo and his three generals—Allende, Aldama, and Jiminez—were captured, and executed at Chiahuahua, and their heads were brought to Guanajuato and hung upon the four corners of the prison. Ten years after Mexico succeeded in throwing off the Spanish yoke. Then the Mexicans carried the heads of their heroes to the Capital, and with loving rites laid them under the Altar of the Kings in the great Cathedral. Hidalgo, the Romish priest, the Mexican, has the New England type of face—the same type we see in the signers of our own constitution. It is the face of both a dreamer and a doer, an enthusiast as well as a man of judgment.

Unlike Zacetecas, Guanajuato has a plentiful

water supply, and the town is fresh and blooming. The water is taken from a reservoir—a marvelous piece of engineering—in the mountains above the city. Up the cañon, down which flows the stream from the reservoir, are the homes of the higher classes. Many of the houses are built over the water, and, with their bowering vines, they are enchanting. Through the open doorways we could catch glimpses of flower-decked courts and noble stairways with balustrades of marble or bronze. The churches of Guanajuato are, with the exception of the Cathedral, uninteresting, although in one of them we saw an exquisite copy of Correggio's Holy Night.

The crowd that passes the central plaza in Guanajuato is a motley one, but the American and English elements are almost entirely wanting. This is truly the land of "Grandfather's Hat," for one generation after another succeeds to the treasured headgear. In its holy crown the wearer carries all the germs collected through long ages, besides some other things—a bottle of pulque, some sandals or a cold lunch. If he is fortunate enough to possess two or more sombreros he piles one on top of the other, and travels around like an animated Chinese pagoda.

All day long in the hot sunshine the endless procession marches by, the men, in spite of the fervent

MEXICAN VISTAS 73

CORNER OF THE PLAZA, GUANAJUATO.

heat, hugging themselves in their gay serapes, and the women, who come to fill their water jars at the fountain, twisting their rebosas around their heads. At intervals a Mexican dandy goes by, wearing a gayly embroidered felt sombrero, his bulky shoulders and broad hips sharply defined by his short, tight-fitting jacket, and his revolver-decked sash oddly topping legs of superhuman tenuity. Priests, with worn dark faces, marked with the blue line of the shaven beard, mutter their prayers to the summer sky, the lottery venders cry their wares in high, shrill voices, beggars wrapped in rags demand alms of the passer-by; and every one—beggar, peon, priest, and dandy—lifts his peaked hat reverently as he passes the door of the holy Cathedral.

CHAPTER VII.

Querétaro, as all the world knows, is the opal town. When, upon our arrival, we descended from the train, we were immediately surrounded by the blanketed venders of the precious stones, none of whom seemed to see the humorous aspect of selling opals in pitch darkness—it was ten o'clock at night —but answered our scoffs with a courteous gravity that was a rebuke to us. Before we could find our baggage all the street cars and carriages had disappeared, and we were obliged to walk to the hotel, a distance of more than a mile. Not a single light was visible as we peered down the lonely road, but we hunted up an uncommunicative peon to carry our handbags, and with stout hearts started on our solitary way. It soon proved, however, to be by no means solitary, for a ragged escort sprung up, seemingly from the dust of the road, and attended us, begging, protesting, jabbering. When the attentions of our staff became too oppressive, policemen with lighted lanterns miraculously appeared upon the scene, and, one going before and one following, lighted us for a short distance on our way.

These sudden appearances and disappearances half frightened, half encouraged us. If they conveyed to us a hint of the danger of our night walk, they also assured us that we were carefully looked after.

It seemed to me that we waded through deep sand and stumbled over sharp rocks for half the night; but we came, at last, to a dim plaza, lighted by flaring lamps. Our guide suddenly turned down a dark, narrow street, and, although visions of midnight robbers and assassins danced before our suspicious eyes, we stumbled after him. We entered a low doorway, crossed an unlighted court, groped our way up a perfectly dark stairway, and at last came to a blank, black space, from whose depths a gruff voice cried in Spanish, "No rooms." I uttered an exclamation of horror, but Ahasuerus assured me that there was another hotel, and we plunged down again into the street. We crossed the dimly lighted plaza, entered another hole in the wall, and feeling our way with our feet we climbed upward into a great, cold, brick-floored hall, through whose many windows gleamed a faint but blessed starlight. Our guide knocked at a door, and after a great deal of discussion, not entirely amicable, among the inmates of the room, a half-dressed man appeared bearing in his arms a pile of bed linen and towels. He led us into a cheerless room containing three beds, and making up all of them, so that we could have a bed and a half apiece, he placed a forlorn candle on the rusty iron stand, and left us to our slumbers. We piled the furniture against the door, which had no lock, hid our valuables, and in a few minutes forgot our fears in sleep.

We were wakened early in the morning by hideous cries, and looking out we saw that the plaza market, with its vociferous market women, its pottery venders, and opal merchants, was beneath our windows. One of the market women was serving a novel breakfast dish that seemed to fill a long-felt want. It was as thick as molasses, and as black as ink, but from its odor I think it was a beef stew. The eager peons gathered around the vender and, squatting upon the ground, bought and greedily partook of the brew, sopping in it the sour bread which they took from the high crowns of their dirty sombreros. The odor of garlic came in at the windows, and we, ourselves, did not care for any breakfast.

Querétaro will be remembered as the place where Maximilian made his last stand against the Mexican army. There is no tragedy in history more pitiful than that of Maximilian. Deserted by the wily Napoleon, frowned down by the United States, rejected by the Mexicans whose sovereign he wished to be, he suffered his last humiliation when Lopez, a Spaniard and an officer in his own army, opened the city gates to the enemy, and delivered the emperor into the hands of the Mexicans. It was a sorry end for a prince of the house of Hapsburg, a Count of Savoy, a bright and shining light in the court circles of Europe, to die by the edict of a tat-

HILL OF THE BELLS.

terdemalion nation. In vain the United States protested, in vain the heroic Princess Salm-Salm, riding alone one hundred and fifty miles through desert sands, pleaded, upon her knees, for Maximilian's life; Juarez remained firm, and Maximilian was shot. By the side of the blonde Austrian prince, the dark-browed Mexican, Miramon, and the swarthy Indian Mejia, died bravely for the Church and the government they believed to be of God. Had Maximilian lived, he would have been the present heir to the throne of Austria, and he might have spent a long and useful life, with Carlotta, the unfortunate wife whom his untimely death consigned to a mad-house. As I stood on the stony "Hill of the Bells," where Maximilian looked his last upon the world, I was not ashamed of the tears that filled my eyes for a life so wantonly thrown away.

Querétaro is full of Maximilian. The palace in which he and Carlotta lived during the siege of the town is now a museum. There we registered our names in a book upon the table where the emperor's death warrant was signed, with ink from the inkstand used in signing it. We saw the stools upon which Miramon and Mejia sat during the trial—Maximilian was ill and could not be present—the coffin in which the emperor's body was brought back to the palace, and many other relics. During the siege the plaza was Maximilian's favorite resort. From it he watched the contest, and the Mexicans, learning the fact, trained their guns upon the spot. A shattered fountain is shown as the memento of this hostile fire.

Besides its melancholy association with Maximilian's last hours, Querétaro is also famous for its opal mines, its cotton factory, and its aqueduct. I do not know just where the opal mines are; indeed I could not hear of any one who had ever seen an opal mine, or who knew just how, or where, the stones were obtained. It is sufficient for the non-elect to know that there are opal mines somewhere near Querétaro, and that, for a consideration, more or less satisfactory to the purchaser, the gems can be bought by the traveler. Buying Mexican opals is, however, like adopting a baby; it may turn out well and it may not. The only safeguard for an intending purchaser of the precious stones is to engage as traveling companion an expert lapidary.

The Hercules cotton factory in the suburbs of Querétaro is the largest in Mexico. All around the factory, in a climate wonderfully adapted to the raising of cotton, lie waste lands; yet more than half of the cotton used in the manufacture of the fabrics comes from the United States. The aqueduct, whose graceful outlines can be seen long after passing the town, was presented to Querétaro by a public-spirited citizen. It brings water from the mountains several miles away and distributes it to all the public fountains and reservoirs. It is unfortunate that the generous gift is so little appreciated by the people and the city government; certainly Querétaro's inhabitants are dirty and its streets are by no, means clean.

CHAPTER VIII.

One of the interesting sights between Querétaro and the Capital is the great drainage canal of Nochistongo. It is called the drainage canal that does not drain, but it has in its time drained the Mexicans of both life and money. It was begun two hundred years ago. The first few years of the enterprise the lives of 75,000 Indians were sacrificed; but in spite of this price paid in blood and brawn, within twenty years of the beginning of the canal, the City of Mexico was overflowed to the depth of three feet, and the streets were passable only in boats. This flood lasted five years, and the Spanish king ordered the city to be removed to the higher ground near Chapultepec, but the order was never carried out. At the present day the canal, one of the greatest engineering works in the world, an enterprise which was begun by the celebration of masses, and with the blessing of the Church, is one of the magnificent ruins of Mexico.

It was not yet daylight when we crossed the double rim of the valley of Mexico, and saw before us in the pink dawn the fairy basin with its shining lakes and its snow-crowned mountains. A short whirl through garden-like villages, and we were in the Capital. Our first introduction to the city of the old Aztecs could hardly be considered satisfactory. The town was crowded by an excursion party, and the few hotels were full. We drove to the Hotel Jardin in a cloud of dust raised by the brooms of the street-sweepers, and incidentally we were "dampened down" by the watering pots of the street-sprinklers. We were not therefore in a humor to view with favor the impossible rooms offered for our consideration by the urbane landlord of the Jardin. After applying fruitlessly at the Sanz, the Iturbide, and the Hotel del Opera, we were so fortunate at last as to find shelter at the Coliséo, where we had an elevator, electric lights, hot and cold water, and a charming balcony opening from our parlor upon the street. We have the pleasantest remembrances of the Coliséo, and always upon our return to the Capital we sought its friendly roof. Within two minutes' walk of the hotel there are three good French restaurants and numberless cafés.

Public transit in the City of Mexico is cheap, and fairly comfortable. The intricacies of the streetcar lines are easily mastered. They all start from the principal plaza, and return there. The first-class cars are painted yellow, the second-class green. In both classes of cars the men and often the women smoke continually, so that one who is sickened by tobacco smoke would do well to avoid them. The funeral cars, which are painted black or white, have a sad interest for strangers. The Mexican public carriages carry little tin flags, blue for the first-class, red for the second, and yellow for the third. As the first-class cabs become antiquated they drop in grade to second and finally to third class. The blue-flag cabs, which charge 75 cents a trip, or $1.50 an hour, are as good as the best public carriages in New York or Chicago. The red-flag cabs, price 50 cents a trip, or $1 an hour, are fairly clean and comfortable, while the yellow-flag cabs, 25 cents a trip, or 75 cents an hour, are the cheapest and the shabbiest things in Mexico.

We were in the Capital at the time of the destruction of the Maine. The Mexicans, as a nation, sympathized with the United States, and the jubilee over the affair held by the Spanish clubs was sternly frowned down by the general public. Nevertheless a large sum of money was sent by Spanish sympathizers to Spain, and the largest contributor to the fund was the landlord of a hotel which had been best patronized by the Americans all winter. American money does really "talk," but sometimes it talks on the wrong side.

A STREET IN THE CAPITAL.

From politics to shopping is a sudden jump, but none too sudden for my agile sex. A day or two before our departure for Mexico Ahasuerus found me standing with a puzzled air before the empty trunks. "What are you doing?" he inquired, marveling. "Why don't you pack up?" "I don't know what to pack," I answered, disconsolately. "That's soon settled," he responded. "Take every garment we own, and then we can buy what we need in the City of Mexico." Ahasuerus, as you see, is an old traveler, but for once his experience was at fault. As I foolishly followed his advice and neglected to stock up with the many trifles necessary to a tourist in a warm climate, I was always short of supplies, for I never found those shops so vaunted of the guide books, that are "equal to anything in Paris, London and New York." Doubtless the resident in Mexico who speaks the language fluently, knows where to go and understands the Mexican goods, can shop successfully; but for everything imported he will be obliged to pay at least as much as in the United States. Only native products are cheap in Mexico, and the soul of woman yearns for something besides drawn-work, feather-work, and Mexican pottery.

One of the best things in the City of Mexico is the Mexican Herald—a practical, wide-awake, philanthropic newspaper. Last winter it was making a brave stand for the work of the Humane Society, whose half-dozen members were fighting for the woefully wronged dumb creatures of Mexico. The puny, wailing, wan-eyed babies, the bleeding-backed burros, and the cruelly bitted and spurred horses, sicken and appall the tender heart. The Mexicans are sinfully prolific, yet out of a family of a dozen or fifteen children not more than a third attain maturity. A large percentage of these poor innocents is consequently soon out of misery, but who can estimate the sum of suffering endured by a long-lived animal like the burro? The Herald says, and with justice, that it is impossible to influence Mexicans to treat animals kindly so long as they see American women, who claim to be not only civilized but philanthropic, crowd to the bull-rings and applaud the performance. It is a well-known fact, and Mexicans are not slow to appreciate it, that bull-fights are often gotten up for the amusement of the great excursion parties. The people of the United States should not forget that in this matter they are their "brothers' keepers," and clearly have a responsibility toward their neighbors.

Besides the professional bull-rings and cock-pits, which exist in every Mexican city, and to which admittance can be gained by every one who pays a small fee, there is a growing fashion among the clubs and societies of organizing amateur bull-fights. These are society functions and are attended by the fashionables only. Both the professional and amateur toreadors are generally men, but among the excitements of last winter were the achievements of the "señorita (young lady) bull-fighters." These women contrived by slow degrees to mangle and kill the hapless creatures pitted against them. The horrifying spectacle was taken by the audience as a good joke, and the admiring public flung balls of darning cotton and spools of thread at the fair señoritas instead of the usual offering of cigarettes.

One of the most popular places of amusement in the City of Mexico is Orrin's Circus, where everything in the line of theatricals, from the minstrels to light opera, is presented. It is perfectly respectable and well-managed, and is a proper resort for women and children. The fashionable thêater is the National, but the Theatro Principal is the favorite place of entertainment. As in Cuba, one buys tickets, not for the whole play, but for one act only. After the first act, the buyer is free to leave, or to buy again, as best pleases him. This sampling of theatrical presentations has much to recommend it to our own theater goers, who must often remain through wearisome acts, or lose the money they have invested.

My first experience in theater going in the Capital was an unhappy one. I went, as I should have gone at home, without head covering, for it never occurred to me, in that land of lace mantillas and rebosas, to do otherwise; but, to my confusion, I found myself conspicuous as the only unbonneted woman in the house. The Americans who complain so bitterly of the big hat nuisance in the theaters would be miserable in Mexico, where the women wear the most enormous picture hats I ever beheld. As usual their faces were powdered to ghastliness, and they had a tawdry, overdressed air, but at least there were no bleached blondes among them, for the Spanish women all wear their own pretty black hair, which forms the proper frame for their dark, handsome faces; although, for some reason, doubtless on account of the dry air of the plateau, the tresses of the Mexicans, which are of the same beautiful blue-black color as those of the Cubans, are not so abundant.

On this occasion of our first visit to the theater, as the performance was execrable, we were ready to go at the end of the first act. The orchestra, had it chosen to play good music, was not so bad; but none of the company could sing, and our knowledge of Spanish was not sufficient for us to enjoy the repartee which seemed to delight the audience. In consideration of the unsatisfactory nature of the play, it is, perhaps, hardly patriotic to mention the fact that the actors, although they spoke Spanish fluently, had distinctly the air of Americans, and we were convinced that the basso was a Georgian negro. With the exception of this basso, the actors and the audience were all white.

When I related the story of my blunder in going to the theater without headgear to a sympathizing American woman, who has lived for many years in Mexico, she soothed me with the assurance that if I had gone the next night, I should probably have seen many uncovered heads. "They take their cue from the Americans," she said. "Doubtless the last party of American excursionists who visited the theater wore bonnets, a fashion which no American until now has nullified by example." Although this comforting opinion healed my wounded feelings, I could not wholly accept it. The Mexican women have entirely too good an eye for the pretty coquetries of dress to depend for their models upon their neighbors. If this be a true view of the case, however, the stray American woman must certainly feel a crushing sense of responsibility in regard to headgear and other righteous examples.

CHAPTER IX.

If the traveler would thoroughly understand the City of Mexico he should have an intimate acquaintance with her history and be able to picture in imagination her ancient conditions. Cortés found the Capital floating, like Venice, upon the water, the houses supported by piles resting upon the bed of Lake Texcoco. According to Prescott, the city of 300,000 inhabitants was solidly and handsomely built, and was traversed by three main causeways of cemented rock. These causeways were intersected by canals, crossed by bridges. But Mexico no longer sits, like a huge water-fowl, upon the bosom of the lake. Owing to the great drainage canal, and to natural evaporation, the shores of Lake Texcoco have receded, and are now nearly three miles from the city; so that Mexico is compelled to float, if she floats at all, upon her smells. Certainly they are strong enough to bear her up. These omnipresent smells do not come from the streets, which are really kept clean, but from the houses, whose sewers empty into the gutters. The city, from its situation in the very bottom of the basin, with the water lying always within three feet of the surface, must naturally be unhealthy. Great things are, however, expected from the new drainage canal, which, it is hoped, will do away with the unsanitary conditions.

As you will remember, Cortés was received with kindness by the Aztec emperor, Montezuma, who, in spite of the protests of his heir, Guatemotzin, and the murmurs of the people, loaded the Spaniard with gifts and marks of favor. The Spaniard, true to his nature, repaid the gentle monarch with insolence, robbery, and imprisonment. Montezuma, betrayed and heartbroken, died in six months, and Guatemotzin drove the invaders from the city. The Spaniards took their flight along the main causeway, but the bridges had been broken down and the canal was filled with the barges of the infuriated caciques. The cavaliers, weighed down by their armor and the treasure of gold and silver which they were endeavoring to carry out of the city with them, proved an easy prey to the exasperated Aztecs, who, in those few moments of mad slaughter, avenged the insults and the cruelties of many months.

Along this main causeway, down which the Spaniards fled, and which is now one of the principal streets of the city, are many points of historic interest. At the head of the causeway is the Alameda, or the great city Park. The spot was, in the time of Montezuma, the Indian market place. Later on, in the time of the Viceroys, it was the place for the execution of criminals and the burning of heretics, and the Church of San Diego, at the west end of the park, was approved by an old writer as giving a "beautiful view of the burning place." The Alameda, with its flower plots and sparkling fountains, gives no hint of the former horrors enacted there; nevertheless there is a blot even now upon its beauty—the fine building erected by the Mexican government where the government lotteries are drawn. It is too much, perhaps, to hope that a Spanish-American will ever cease to be a gambler. At all events the United States will find the question a serious one in dealing with their new possessions—for Mexicans, Cubans, Porto Ricans, and doubtless Filipinos also are born gamblers.

As we stroll down the causeway we pass "Alvarado's Leap," the spot where one of the brave lieutenants of Cortés, finding the bridge down and all hope of escape cut off, to the awe and admiration of the pursuing foe, jumped the chasm. History does not record the exact length of this jump, but it is described as beyond human possibility. Nevertheless Alvarado's conduct, both before and after this feat, is a guarantee that he was extremely human. Further down the causeway, where the loss of Spanish life was heaviest, is the pretty Church of the Martyrs, where masses are continually said for the dead. The spot is easily identified by the smells, for the dead and gone martyrs—or some of the living ones—still taint the air. Nevertheless the church is an interesting one, and contains some particularly fine copies of Murillo's Holy Family of the National Gallery, and the Immaculate Conception of the Louvre. Near the Church of the Martyrs is a monument to the patriot Morelos, the last victim of the Inquisition in Mexico. When we remember that Morelos was executed in 1814, almost within the memory of living men, the Inquisition seems very near to us.

The Mexican Pantheon—the Church of San Fernande—is also situated upon the causeway. In the little Campo Santo attached to San Fernande lie many of Mexico's greatest men. Here sleeps Juarez, under a marble canopy, entirely covered with bead wreaths. The monument of the great president is a figure of the Republic, holding in her arms the dying hero. This beautiful work of art, one of the very finest in Mexico, is by the brothers Yslas, who have shown a true appreciation of their subject. Other patriots who lie in San Fernande are Morelos, Guerrero, and Zaragossa. Miramon and Mejia are also buried there, but there are no bead wreaths on their tombs, for Mexico, although she may forgive her enemies, does not honor them. Maximilian, who died with Miramon and Mejia, lies in the beautiful castle of Miramir on the Adriatic. In front of San Fernande, in the pretty park, is a monument to Guerrero, one of Mexico's favorite heroes.

At the end of the causeway, in the village of Tlacopan, now called Tacuba, is the great tree under which Cortés sat down and wept. All seemed lost; he had burned his ships, and every hope of escape was cut off. He was surrounded by an enraged foe; of his little army only a handful remained, and his heart sickened as he thought of the horrible fate of his captive comrades, reserved for the sacrificial fires of the Aztecs. Well might it be for Cortés a "sad night."

If the reader knows his Prescott as he should—for, whether authentic or not, it is a marvelous story—he knows that, in the end, the Spaniards were sufficiently strong and wily to conquer the country and make of it a Spanish province. Consequently it is the mixed blood of Spaniard and Indian which flows in the veins of the Mexican of to-day. This half-breed is not born to the inheritance of joyousness that the Cuban is, whose few drops of negro blood put quicksilver into his nature. The Mexican has all the pomposity of the Spaniard and all the stolidity of the Indian. He wraps himself in his graceful serape and with a stately "Pardon me" walks the earth, believing himself its master. It is true that the upper classes in the Mexican cities have adopted the American dress—or some modification of it—but they keep all the old-time stately ceremonials of the Spaniard.

The hospitality of these lordly persons is almost oppressive. When the stranger enters a house, he is assured by his host, "It is yours, Señor, accept it"—and his it remains—in the assurance of the free-handed Don—as long as he chooses to stay, albeit his soul is never gladdened by the sight of the title deeds properly signed and registered. The same apparent generosity is shown in the matter of furniture, horses, and jewels. If the stranger admires a pin, a ring, a cane, "It is yours," again exclaims the gracious Mexican, and he urges its acceptance in terms so pressing that the admirer is at loss for words to refuse the proffered gift. But woe to the practical American who mistakes this pretense for real generosity. A certain countryman of ours, who had most unwillingly accepted a horse that was fairly forced upon him, because he no longer dared refuse it, was made aware of his mistake in the most disagreeable manner. "What sort of a man is that friend of yours?" inquired the donor of an acquaintance of the recipient. "He must be a thief; he has taken my horse."

Every social relation, even the most ordinary forms of courtesy, is tinctured with this ceremonious insincerity. To the traveler the Mexican bows and grimaces, which mean nothing at all, are, at first, amazing. I watched one day in a horse car an interesting play. As two young men entered the car, one of them hastened to pay the fare for both, and presented his companion with the ticket. The companion, with a start of horror, and any amount of hand-waving and protests, refused it, and when he was, at last, prevailed upon to accept the favor, he did it with a succession of salaams and hat-liftings that made my neck ache. The recipient of the ticket then produced his cigarette case and proffered its contents to his friend, who, after many stately genuflexions, consented to take one. They then lighted their cigarettes, and vigorously puffed the smoke into my face. However, a saturation of tobacco smoke is an advantage in a country infested with moths, and the Mexican cigarettes are so delightfully fragrant that I had no fault to find with them. On the contrary, when an American, who wished to be very Spanish indeed, puffed the smoke of a strong, fat cigar in my eyes I resented it, even in Mexico. The Mexican women smoke as much as the men, and many of the smokers seem to belong to the better class; certainly they are not of the same class as the women smokers in France, whose example American women and girls sometimes make the mistake of imitating.

One who likes black eyes may have a surfeit of them in Mexico, for every one, from prince to peon, has beautiful dark orbs with curling, jetty lashes. Their languishing, sideways glances were, at first, very fascinating to me, but I soon tired of them, and in the end, even learned to distrust them. I had an adventure one evening that convinced me that the Mexican eyes are not the ones to inspire confidence in an emergency. I left the Hotel Coliséo, intending to meet Ahasuerus at the restaurant two or three blocks away, and, with my usual fatal facility for wandering, took the wrong turn, and soon found that I was lost. As the streets change their names every block, the street signs gave me no hint of my whereabouts, and, for once, the ubiquitous policeman was nowhere in sight. I wandered for an hour, and as it was getting dark, I began to be troubled. I looked at the ragged peons, and the gallant, black-eyed señors without any desire to address them, but I finally accosted a pretty French señorita, who, with her Indian maid, was hurrying like a frightened pigeon through the lighted streets. She, however, knew nothing of the city, and her directions sent me far afield.

All at once I espied, in the door of a shop, a familiar gray figure, with a sideways tilted hat, and hands in trousers pockets. I walked confidently up to the figure and said, "Pardon me; I see that you are an American. Can you direct me to the Hotel Coliséo?" The stranger looked right at me with his honest eyes—I don't know what color they were, but they were straightforward American eyes—gave me the required directions plainly and concisely, and touched his hat respectfully as I walked off, blessing the honest American eyes and the big American heart to which neither child nor woman fears to appeal.

Upon reaching the hotel I found Ahasuerus anxiously pacing up and down on the lookout for me. When I told him the story of my adventure he exclaimed, "Well, of all stupids I ever did see! Why on earth didn't you call a cab, and ask to be driven to the Coliséo?" And when I turned and looked at him little spurts of bright flame seemed to burst out, like a halo, all around his head, and then and there I fell down and worshiped the giant intellectuality, the unfathomable resource, of the American man.

CHAPTER X.

One of the interesting places in the City of Mexico, both on account of its beauty and for the historical associations connected with it, is the Cathedral. It is built upon the spot where formerly stood the old Aztec teocalli, or temple, in which the Indians offered sacrifices to their gods. The present building, which is upon the site of a former church, was erected in 1573, and is therefore 325 years old. It is of grand dimensions, but the beauty and the impressiveness of the interior are marred—as in most Mexican churches—by the choir, which is placed in the nave, and by the high altar, which is clumsy and inartistic. This altar is, at present, being redecorated with barbaric gilding and florid colors. Under the flashy altar of Los Reyes are buried the heads of Hidalgo, Allende, Aldama, and Jiminez, which were brought here from the prison hooks of Guanajuato. These men were excommunicated by the Catholic Church as heretics and traitors, and I do not know how the ecclesiastics explain their burial on consecrated ground. The radical party in the republic wish the remains of the patriots to be interred elsewhere, and as soon as a suitable place can be provided doubtless that wish will be carried out. Under a neighboring altar lie the remains of the first emperor, Iturbide—called by his grateful countrymen the Liberator. These same grateful countrymen, by the way, did not forget to bestow upon him the reward of the Mexican liberator—death. Here at the great altar near which he lies the first emperor was crowned, and from the same spot, forty years after, Maximilian, that royal usurper, followed him along the road to death. From the same altar, a few years later, the triumphant government of Juarez took, for the aid of republican principles, the gold candlesticks and the gold and jeweled statue of the Assumption.

In the chapter house is a Madonna said to be by Murillo. In spite of my doubts, a sight of the picture convinced me of its authenticity. No one but Murillo could paint so adorable a baby. The peaceful mother holds the dimpled child in her strong, tender arms, while he, baby-fashion, springs toward the little St. John at the Virgin's knee. Over them all, with love in her old face, broods St. Anne. There are several other fairly good pictures in the Cathedral, but one—by the woman artist, La Somaya—which the guide-books extol, we could not find, and the sacristan seemed to know nothing of it.

The little zocalo or plaza beside the Cathedral is bright with flowers and fountains, and gay with the passing crowds. It is a good place to sit and hear the band play, to study Mexican types, and to listen to the boom of the great Cathedral bell, Santa Maria Guadalupe. This bell, which is nineteen feet long, is, with the exception of the cracked Kremlin bell of Moscow, the biggest one in the world. Santa Maria Guadalupe, however, is not cracked, and it has the further advantage of being in a climate where one can sit outside every day in the year and listen to its deep tones.

While you are in the mood for seeing pictures, living and on canvas, it is a good time to visit the old Academy of San Carlos, which is now the Museum of Art, and which claims to have in its collection pictures by Murillo, Velasquez, Rubens and Van Dyke. Some of the older Mexican artists, particularly Ibarra, who lived early in the seventeenth century, seem to have had no little feeling for art, but the modern delight too much in gay coloring, and strong shading; nevertheless many of the historical paintings are very interesting. The sculptures in the gallery, with the exception of the model of Juarez' monument by the Yslas brothers, are casts of Greek statuary.

The first time we went to the National Museum we were accosted by a guide who offered to reveal to us the mysteries of the collection for the modest sum of five dollars. When we offered him one dollar he accepted it, however, and seemed perfectly satisfied. It was certainly a dollar well invested, for he proved to be an intelligent man, who, strangely enough for a guide, really knew what he was talking about.

The most curious thing in the Museum is the Calender stone of the Aztecs, which was found near the present site of the Cathedral. Archeologists now believe it to have been the base of the smaller sacrificial stone. Upon this sacrificial stone, which is curiously carved, and which is cut by a channel, down which flowed the blood of the victim to the vase beneath, perished annually from twenty to fifty thousand persons. The Museum contains troops of Aztec gods; Chac-Mool, the very unpleasant god of fire; the well-known "Indio-Triste" (Sad Indian), who is anything but sad, some very realistic serpents, and several vases for holding the sacred fire. The hieroglyphics, and the picture dispatches sent to Montezuma announcing the coming of the Spaniards, are most interesting. On the second floor are the natural history exhibits, which are much like those of other Museums. The third floor is devoted to portraits and mementos of Mexico's great

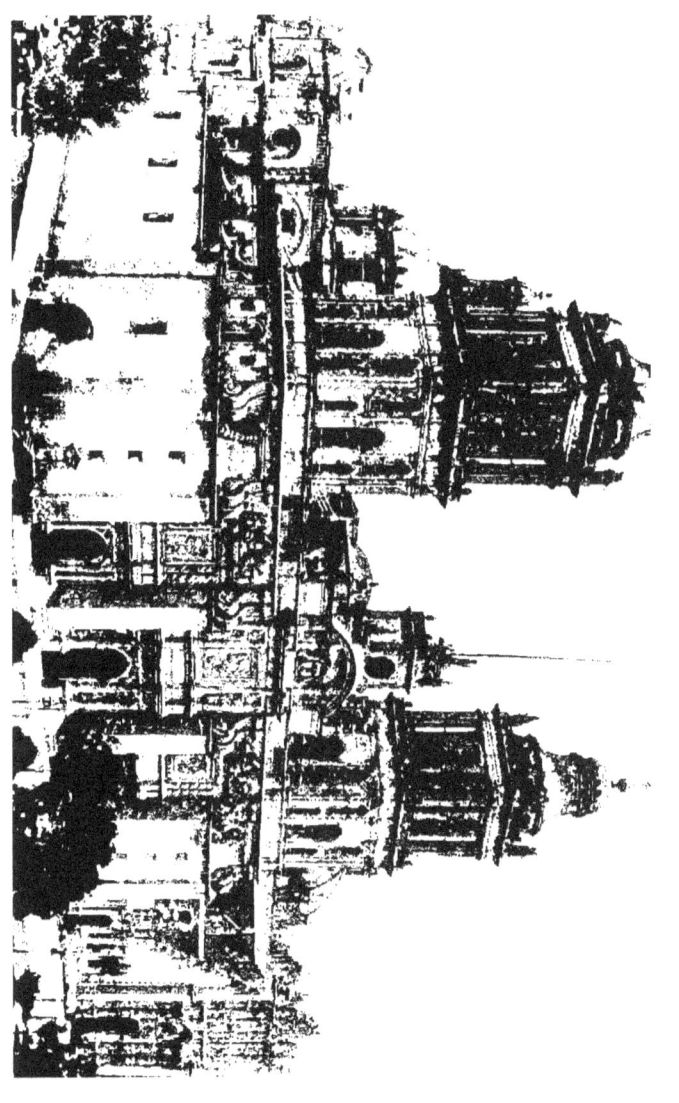

men. There is a portrait of Cortés, with the narrow head and sly eyes of a schemer and a bigot, and one of the blonde Maximilian, who, judging from his face, was not born for stormy times. Alvarado's armor, Hidalgo's standard, and Maximilian's plate and state carriage, are also exhibited. There are likewise humble souvenirs of Juarez, of Hidalgo, and of Morelos, their candle-sticks, their shabby garments—pathetically homely objects of daily use —which should be sacredly guarded from curious eyes. To me it seems as indelicate to display these homely objects of personal belonging as to read a man's love letters or to spy upon his prayers.

Near the National Museum is the National Palace, sometimes used by the President as a dwelling. It is official headquarters, and in the reception hall those who are fortunate enough to have letters to the President are generally received. Although the palace was, at one time, the abode of the luxurious Carlotta, the apartments are by no means magnificent, but the grand drawing-room and the study of the little Porfirio Diaz are interesting. The great reception hall should be called a mortuary chapel, for it is hung with the portraits of Mexico's heroes, most of whom have died violent deaths. On the wall hangs also an immense painting of the battle of Cinco de Mayo—fifth of May. This battle, which was fought on the hills back of Puebla, determined the fate of Maximilian. At one end of the reception hall, on a raised dais, is the presidential chair, upholstered in velvet and gold and with the gilt eagle of Mexico above it. The whole apartment has much the air of a European throne-room, and the man who fills the presidential chair of Mexico is more potent than many continental sovereigns.

In the vicinity of the Cathedral is the Monte de Piedad, or national pawn-shop. This is a practical and beneficent charity, by means of which people in straits are enabled to obtain just rates on objects pledged. The owners of the property are given a specified time for redemption, but if unredeemed the articles are put on sale for the price of the loan. At the end of each month the price of the pledges is marked down, so that people who wish to purchase a certain article, can, by waiting a few months, buy at reasonable rates if the desired articles remain unsold. The Monte de Piedad is a sad place, filled with the wrecks of broken homes and shattered fortunes. Common household utensils, pianos, tawdry garments, valuable jewels, old saddles, painted fans, broken furniture, and point lace jostle one another, and hopelessly confuse the intending purchaser as to values. Nevertheless tourists may sometimes pick up at the Monte de Piedad valuable articles for reasonable prices, but so-called bargains are not common. During the administration—or rather lack of administration—of Diaz' predecessor, President Gonzales, the Monte de Piedad suffered with other government institutions, and narrowly escaped bankruptcy. President Diaz has, however, put all government interests on a stable and, let us hope, a lasting basis.

AZTEC WOMAN WITH DISTAFF.

CHAPTER XI.

Sunday morning all the Mexican world goes to the Church Parade in the Alameda. This function is less hilarious and, I think, in better taste than the London Church Parade, for the Mexicans seem very conscious of the absurdity of the whole affair; in fact, they have an air of being ashamed of themselves. Although most of the promenaders wear the American dress the crowd does not represent, as in London, the aristocracy of the city. The women, who are by no means as handsome as the pretty Cubans with their flirting fans and enticing mantillas, have a most execrable fashion of powdering their faces until they look like dough-balls; and I was not impressed with their escorts—the tiny warriors—who did not look as if they would be very terrible soldiers. It would seem that the Indian strain is less vigorous, as well as less joyous, than the negro, for I was struck with the sloping shoulders, narrow chests, and awkward carriage of both sexes. Indeed, I should think that a teacher of Delsarte would be in demand in Mexico. Still, in spite of their physical defects, the Mexican soldiers have shown that they can fight, although Ahasuerus, who is authority on military matters, declares that they do not know how to stand properly, or how to hold their guns.

One Sunday morning, as we came from the Parade, we were met at the park entrance by a multitude of excited people, fleeing before the horses of mounted policemen, and before we could realize the situation, we were in the midst of a howling mob. To escape the crowd, which was hurling itself from the opposite direction upon us, and to avoid being trampled under the feet of the police horses, we climbed upon the pedestal of one of the big tigers at the park entrance. In vain we sought from our neighbors an explanation of this, to us, utterly incomprehensible excitement. No one heeded our inquiries, and we ourselves could see no cause for the outbreak, although we noticed that the fury of the rabble seemed to be concentrated upon a band of mild-mannered and trembling mandolin players, who formed the center of the mob, and who were evidently under the protection of the police. An article in one of the papers, a few days later, explained the mystery. It seems that Mexico, unlike most capital cities, strongly objects to innovations. So strong, indeed, is this sentiment that the first bicyclists who appeared upon the streets of the city narrowly escaped injury at the hands of the mob. The unfortunate musicians whom we saw were guilty, first, of introducing mandolin playing upon the streets, and, secondly, of being Spaniards, which was, in those days of the wrecked Maine, an offense in the eyes of the republic-loving Mexicans. For ourselves the result of this experience was to give us an added respect for the strong man at the head of the Mexican government, who holds in check a people so excitable and so turbulent.

Sunday afternoon, from four to seven o'clock, the fashionable world drives on the Paseo, and here one sees elegant equipages, and beautiful, high-bred women. Down each side of the broad roadway extends a line of motionless troopers, sitting on their horses as if carved in bronze, and under their outstretched swords the carriages pass in line. The rigid position must be torture for the soldiers, but the ceremony gives a military and official air to the promenade. Although a fashionable function, the Sunday drive is not confined to the fashionables, and the poorer Mexicans will deny themselves the comforts of life for the whole week that they may save the needful money to hire a carriage for the drive on the popular promenade.

The Paseo extends from the little plaza of Charles IV. to the palace of Chapultepec, a distance of about two miles. It was laid out by Carlotta in imitation of the Champs-Elysées of Paris, and, like the Champs-Elysées, has several garden-like rond-points, or glorietas. The street is kept very clean by constant sprinklings with watering pots. Along the sides of the roadway are statues of Mexican patriots and rows of carved stone benches, from which one can watch the Sunday procession of gay carriages.

In the matter of public monuments the United States must look to her laurels, for in this respect Mexico bids fair to outstrip her. At the head of the Paseo stands the grand equestrian statue of Charles IV. of Spain, modeled after the statue of Marcus Aurelius at Rome. The Spanish monarch was no favorite in Mexico, but as a work of art the monument is allowed to remain. In another glorieta is the spirited figure of the young Columbus, and still further on that of the heroic Guatemotzin, the heir of Montezuma, and last of the Aztec emperors. A bas-relief upon the pedestal represents the torture by Cortés of the Indian prince, and other incidents in his career. The figure of the young monarch is strong and fearless, but the attentive face seems already to foresee its doom. The cruel conqueror of the last of the Aztec royal line died in Spain. His body was brought back to Mexico for burial, but after the independence of the country was proclaimed it was found necessary, in order to save the bones from the fury of the people, to return them to Spain. Montezuma and Guatemotzin are household words in their native land, but there is in all Mexico no monument to Cortés, and no street nor city bears his name. Once again, posterity gives a righteous verdict.

HILL AND CASTLE OF CHAPULTEPEC.

The Paseo ends at the palace of Chapultepec, the beautiful home of the Mexican rulers. The present palace is built upon the site of Montezuma's summer home, and under the shade of its dark cypresses the melancholy prince often brooded over the encroachments of the Spaniards, and the fate that was before his people and himself. Chapultepec was, also, at a later day, the favorite residence of Cortés, and its woods are said to be haunted by the spirit of his Indian mistress, the gentle Marina. It is believed by the Mexicans that her shadowy form may be seen at twilight, flitting through the woods and gardens that she loved. It would seem but justice that this punishment should be reserved for her, that she should come back to look upon the degradation of her own race, whom, for the love of a stranger, she betrayed and deserted.

The hill of Chapultepec, or Grasshopper Hill, upon which stands the castle, was besieged and taken by the American army in the Mexican war. The fortress was bravely defended by the boy cadets of Mexico, and a monument to the memory of the young heroes is erected at the foot of the hill. Since those dreadful days we have had an opportunity to show our friendship for Mexico, but at the grave of these little lads every true American must feel a tender contrition. Chapultepec, besides being the home of the president, is also the West Point of Mexico. The young cadets whom we saw strolling around, with their books under their arms, were pretty, bright-eyed, courteous boys, with modest and unaffected bearing—doubtless just such boys as those silent ones, who sleep below.

The view from the heights of Chapultepec is one of the famous ones of the world. The lovely valley of Mexico, with its shimmering lakes, its snow-capped volcanoes, its white-walled towns and villages, and its historic battlefields, lies at the feet of the gazer. No one, looking down on that picture of fairy land, could possibly imagine that such a thing as an evil smell or a dirty street was ever known to the favored inhabitants.

For a palace—which in my experience is generally shabby and uncomfortable—Chapultepec is quite satisfactory—in fact, really luxurious. Much of the beautiful furniture and drapery Carlotta brought with her from France. There is, however, one unpleasant feature about Chapultepec, and that is the custodian. Unlike his fellow-countrymen in general, he is not in the least courteous, and he seems to regard all Americans with suspicion. Indeed, although as a nation we are admired by our neighbors, I think that as individuals we are not in particularly good favor with the Mexicans; and perhaps we should not marvel at their adverse judgment of us. When we seriously reflect upon the American occupation of foreign cities we cannot censure our neighbors for their criticisms. They judge us as we judge them, from what they see, and one who has traveled much must acknowledge that their strictures are often just. We crowd their revered ruins and their sacred art galleries with irreverent feet and chattering tongues, and treat their people as strange and amusing spectacles. We are so persuaded that our cars, our steam-heat and our overloaded hotel tables are the last triumph of civilization that we endeavor to impose our belief in their merits upon the world at large. And there are even worse offenses. The custodian at Chapultepec told us that a party of Americans who had lately visited the place had cut the velvet tassels from the elegant hangings in Señora Diaz' boudoir. We saw the mutilated hangings and were forced to blush for our countrywoman—for only a woman could have committed such an outrage.

Fortunately we have the remedy for all these things in our own hands, and I am sure that I am safe in predicting that it will not be long before the American woman will be acknowledged abroad as the model of courtesy and honor. I suppose we must be resigned to rest, however, for all time under the ban of pious conservatives, like the sweet-faced old señora whom I saw one day in the City of Mexico. The señora, who, from her lace mantilla, evidently belonged to the old régime, entered the street car in which I was a passenger, seated herself beside me, looked me straight in the face, examined me minutely from top to toe, then crossed herself several times and began to patter prayers under her breath. Doubtless she considered me as a dangerous creature, one of the great army of American adventurers, mineholders, railway and telegraph builders who are seeking to overturn the good old ways of Mexico.

Fortunately not all Mexicans are of the señora's way of thinking. President Porfirio Diaz is as intelligent and as progressive as the best American. Under his wise rule Mexico is taking great strides forward, and it is to be hoped that his days may be long in the land. The most popular woman in the country is Señora Diaz, the sweet-faced wife of the president. This simply attired, gracious wife of a great ruler is a thorough gentlewoman. She received us with the most graceful courtesy, paying us the greatest compliment possible to pay a stranger by addressing us in our own tongue, and I blushed as I responded to her elegant English, knowing that I could not speak fifty words in her own language. Señora Diaz spoke in the kindliest manner of the United States, and I was glad to answer her honestly that we were proud of our young sister republic and anxious to be on sisterly terms with her.

Although Mexico prides herself upon being a republic, and although loyal Mexicans almost always speak of the country as "la republica," and seldom as "Mexico," still the government is not, in our sense of the word, really a republic. Happily for Mexico, the franchise, as we know it, does not exist. The power is vested in a strong government, with a strong man at its head. Diaz has been president for eighteen years. He has continued the wise policy of the great Juarez, and has given to the country railroads, telegraphs, free schools, and libraries. He is the leader of the Liberal party, the party which stands for freedom and enlightenment,

as opposed to the more conservative policy of the
Church. Diaz, who is a half-breed, born in Oaxaca, has been from his youth in military and political
life. He is a man of iron will and tremendous pow-

PRESIDENT DIAZ.

ers of resistance. As an example of his rugged
endurance, a surgeon in the Confederate army related to us that he found Diaz, after one of the
battles of the French invasion, suffering from a

cruel wound, which had been greatly aggravated by the blundering knives of the native surgeons. A severe operation was necessary to save his life, but Diaz refused to take anesthetics, and bore the horrible torture of the operation with hardly a change of countenance. The one blot upon the record of this great soldier is his revolt against Juarez; but his patriotic zeal and his wise administration have blotted that error from the minds of his countrymen, and Diaz stands to-day for all that is best in Mexico. Unfortunately the Church party, fostered by the influence of the clergy and many of the good women of the land, is rapidly increasing in wealth and power. To this party even Señora Diaz, who is a patriotic woman and a devoted wife, is a most loyal adherent.

During the administration of one of Diaz' predecessors, a friend of the General remarked to him, "You will be the next president." "No," replied Diaz, "there will be no next president. By that time I shall be an American citizen"—meaning a citizen of the United States. His prophecy is in a certain sense fulfilled, since he is an American citizen as well as an American ruler, although he has no longer any expectation or desire of becoming a fellow-citizen of ours. Nevertheless he is anxious to imitate our virtues, while eschewing our faults, and to live in amity with us. This was also the dream of the kindly Romero, whose death we are at this moment mourning, and that of Señora Romero, the American wife of one of the best-beloved of all the Mexicans. It is to be hoped that these generous sentiments will become universal and that the two sister republics, side by side, may unite in a kindly emulation for all the triumphs of free religion and civilization.

CHAPTER XII.

When the Spaniards first entered the City of Mexico one of the wonderful sights that met their astonished eyes was "those fairy islands of flowers, overshadowed by trees of considerable size, rising and falling with the gentle undulation of the billows." The chinampas, or floating gardens, thus described by Prescott, were originally formed of frames of osiers filled with the soil from the bottom of the lake, upon the surface of which they floated. Although still beautiful with their wealth of bloom and verdure, the chinampas no longer float, but are anchored along the shores of the canal, and make no pretense to be anything but irrigated fruit and vegetable gardens. From the irrigating ditches barges laden with garden produce are floated into the Viga canal, and thence to the market places of the city.

It was a hot morning when first we strolled slowly through the poorer districts of the Capital, toward the Viga canal. The filth, misery and drunkenness were depressing, but not worse than in many

CANAL DE LA VIGA—*page 118.*

cities of the old world. "This," said a man in clerical garb, addressing us in a ministerial tone, "is the fruit of Romanism." I did not care to remind him that in the Protestant city of Glasgow the scene might be duplicated, and that the Cowgate of that great Presbyterian stronghold, Edinburgh, is infinitely worse. Although I dread, as every friend of the country must, the influence of the Church upon her political conditions, still I have little sympathy for the contempt so freely manifested by some Protestants for the Catholic Church in Mexico. I never see a peasant or a peon kneeling before an altar without feeling glad that he has this staff of comfort to help him on his weary way. Better, a thousand times, is even the grossest superstition, than no belief at all.

The Viga canal, which drains the waters of Lake Xochimilco into the lower level of Lake Texcoco, is no longer the limpid stream that Cortés' army saw. It is now the sewage conduit for the city, and the whole stagnant mass suggests cholera, typhus, and other diseases incident to filth. In these vile waters women were washing their hair and bathing their babies, men were wading, children were paddling, and the whole community seemed to regard the yellow flood as a great advantage. Barges laden with fruits and vegetables were poling down the canal, and great loads of dead pigs—

which, upon investigation, proved to be only pigskins filled with pulque—passed by us on their fragrant way. We knew it was our duty as conscientious tourists also to launch our bark upon the stream, but as we did not care to stir up the sleeping nastiness with a boat we took the horse cars instead. The line passes along one of the three ancient causeways, the one by which the army of Cortés first entered the city. As we go south the track bends beside the stream, the tall trees meet overhead, the crowd lessens, the water clears, and the Viga canal really becomes a thing of beauty. The first town south of Mexico is Santa Anita, the Mexican Coney Island. It is a popular resort on holidays and offers unlimited advantages to gamblers.

There are several ancient and shabby towns with dilapidated churches along the route. The market women, with their scant stores spread around them, sit listlessly under the shade of the trees, and comfortless barges loaded with passengers pass by on their way to Lake Xochimilco and the towns along its shores. At Mexicalcingo the car-line branches, one line continuing south to Xochimilco, the other going east to Ixtapalapan. At Mexicalcingo there is a picturesque old church, smelling of dead and gone saints, and a quaint wayside shrine over which the wild vines climb. We walked

CORTÉS BRIDGE.

over to a romantic stone bridge—the same, tradition has it, to which Montezuma came with his escort to meet the treacherous Cortés and to bid him welcome to the city. It was doubtless on just such a sunny morning as this that the feather-crowned Aztecs welcomed their stern and visored guests, and thus set the seal to their own destruction.

Across this old bridge must have come, too, General Scott with his army. He crossed the mountains where Cortés crossed before him, through the pass between the white volcanoes, marched down the road to the battlefields of Cherubusco and Molino del Rey, which we see yonder, and thence swept on to Chapultepec and the City of Mexico. Independent of its historical associations the old bridge is a pleasant resting place, and we loitered in the sunshine, watching a graceful woman washing clothes in the stream. Fortunately for the welfare of the household linen the water was clearer than nearer the city. Troops of velvet-coated donkeys, almost hidden under their loads of verdant forage, ambled by, and a woman and three children, bearing upon their backs great bundles of cane, passed us with a courteous "Buenos dias, señor; Buenos dias, señora." It seems impossible that a human back—much less the back of a woman or a child—can support such a weight as these people habitually carry. Two hundred and fifty pounds is the average load for the Mexican porter.

If we cross the bridge and continue east along the ancient causeway, we shall come to the old City of Ixtapalapan, the former residence of the brother of Montezuma. In this town Cortés was hospitably received by the prince, Cuitlahua, who accompanied the Spaniards on their way to the Capital. Like Mexico, Ixtapalapan was built upon piles above the water, and was a city of fine architecture and magnificent gardens, all of which excited the too ready cupidity of the Spaniards. The hospitality of Cuitlahua Cortés afterward requited with the blackest ingratitude. When the Spaniards, some months after their expulsion from the City of Mexico, returned again to besiege the Capital, remembering the "noche triste," and burning with a desire to avenge their comrades, they attacked Ixtapalapan. As the battle went against them, the brave inhabitants of the doomed city, seeing that all was lost, cut down the dykes and allowed the waters of the lake to overflow the town. A horrible conflict ensued in which the warriors fought waist-deep in the flood, but the usual good fortune attended the Spaniards, and the massacre that followed the victory is a foul blot on the record of Cortés.

Nothing is left of the stately Aztec city except a little hamlet with a decaying church, and some miraculous volcanic springs. Above the town rises the Mexican Mount of the Holy Cross—the Hill of the Star—whose summit bears an immense cross. This Hill of the Star was formerly a holy hill to the Aztecs. The nation counted time by cycles of fifty-two years. Every time the cycle came to a close the people confidently expected the end of all things, and the last five days of each cycle were spent in wailing and gloom; the sacred fires went out on all the altars, and everything was ready for the coming of the final hour. On the last night of the fifty-second year the priests accompanied by the people repaired to the Hill of the Star, bearing with them the flower of all their captives. At midnight, when the Pleiades reached the zenith, the hapless victim was sacrificed, and upon his body the new fire was kindled. As the flames streamed up into the heavens they were seen by all the watching towns and villages, who immediately broke out into songs of thanksgiving. The rekindling of the sacred fire was regarded by the Aztecs as a prophecy and a pledge that the nation would live and prosper for another cycle.

CHAPTER XIII.

The patron saint of the City of Mexico is Nuestra Señora de los Remedios—Our Lady of Succor. Our Lady of Los Remedios is made of wood, and is only about ten inches long. She has lost one eye and the larger part of her nose, and, as one who is aware of the vicissitudes through which she has passed would expect, is a very shabby and pitiful little saint. She was brought to America by one of Cortés' soldiers, and during the time the Spaniards were entertained by the kindly Montezuma in the Capital, the wooden saint was placed upon a tiny shrine erected upon one of the teocallis. The "noche triste" so fatal to the Spaniards was also an unfortunate night for Our Lady of Los Remedios, for although she was carried by her friends out of the city, she was mislaid in the confusion, and nothing was heard of her for twenty years. At the end of that time Our Lady appeared to a Christian Aztec, who was sleeping on the spot where the Spaniards had camped the night after their expulsion from the Capital, and bade him look under a maguey bush near by, for her lost image. The Indian searched, found the lost saint, and taking it to his home tried to feed it, but it refused to eat, and during the night it fled once more to the shelter of the maguey bush. The Indian brought it back, locked it up in a strong box, and sat on the lid, but the saint returned to her old place, and the Church, seeing that she wished to remain there, built a temple and a shrine on the spot for her; and there she is to-day, a poor, blackened, mutilated little image, holding in her arms a tiny figure of the Christ. Once her altars were decked with silver, gold, and jewels; but all that is gone now, and even the lamps upon the shrine of this impecunious, one-eyed, little saint are of tin. The gourd from which the Indian who found her endeavored to induce her to eat is religiously preserved as a voucher for the authenticity of the story.

It is to Our Lady of Los Remedios that the people appeal in times of drought—albeit the most earnest efforts to provide her own shrine with water have failed. She is also called upon in times of special need, and at the festival of September first she is carried in procession through the city. At the time of the last severe visitation of cholera Our Lady was brought in solemn state to the Cathedral, followed by the Archbishop and all the church dignitaries, and deposited upon the grand altar. But she refused to remain and was found the next day on her own shrine near the maguey bush, her soiled and mud-stained garments showing that she had made the return trip on foot.

Like some others of her sex, the Lady of Los Remedios has greatly impaired her usefulness by entering into politics. During the fight for Mexico's independence, she unfortunately chose the wrong side, and gained the contumely and contempt of the patriots. She held a General's commission in the Spanish army, and with others of her political faith was exiled from the city, but the sentence was never carried out. On account of her political record, however, the Lady of Los Remedios is not a popular saint to-day in Mexico. In order to see her chapel and shrine one must go by the N. R. R. to Naucalpan and climb the hill of Totoltepec on burros.

Fortunately the Mexicans have another saint; one that has no admixture of Spanish blood, no affiliation with the Conquerors—a saint that is all their own. It is not strange that, after the Conquest, even those Aztecs who accepted the faith of the invaders should feel a sullen resentment against the Spanish saints, who from the first had so successfully outgeneraled their gods. The powers which had so loyally aided the Conquerors, could, they thought, be no friends of theirs. It was therefore peculiarly fortunate that the Virgin of Guadalupe appeared at the moment she did.

Upon the hill of Guadalupe was an ancient Aztec temple for the worship of Tonantzin, the mother of all the gods. The Spaniards, according to their wont, destroyed the temple and established near by a mission for the conversion of the Indians. One morning, as a pious Indian convert, Juan-Diego by name—or, in our vernacular, John-James—was returning from mass, he was accosted by a veiled figure which instructed him to go to the Bishop and command him to build a church on the spot where the figure was standing. But the unbelieving Bishop refused to listen to the mandate, and although the veiled figure appeared to the Indian again, and once again, the Bishop still refused to believe the story unless the poor fellow brought some undeniable token that the tale was true. The persevering vision came to Juan-Diego for the fifth time, and when he begged for a sign, it directed him to pick the flowers at his feet. To his surprise he saw the ground beneath him suddenly covered with beautiful blossoms which he proceeded to pluck, and with which he filled his tilma or mantle. The Indian carried the blossoms joyfully to the good Bishop, and when he opened his tilma to show the token, behold on the tilma was imprinted the figure of the Virgin. On the spot where the vision had stood when it first accosted Juan-Diego, a spring of water gushed forth. Over this spring, as well as over the other places where the Virgin had appeared, chapels were built, the shrine of Guadalupe became the haunt of pilgrims and penitents, and in every Mexican church was erected an altar to the new saint.

In spite of the obvious authenticity of the story the Spanish church dignitaries were at first disposed to look rather coldly on this Indian virgin, whom they evidently considered as a "second-rate" saint. Canonization was most grudgingly bestowed upon her, and it was understood among the elect that she was to be considered as a strictly Mexican saint. The great festivals in honor of her first appearance were counted as especially Indian festivals, and the Indians came long distances to lay their gifts on the altar of their own particular Virgin. Some of the scoffing ecclesiastics even went so far as to accuse the poor Mexicans of worshiping, not at the shrine of the Virgin of Guadalupe, but at the altar of their old deity, Tonantzin, the mother of the gods. However, the protection which the Virgin of Guadalupe extended over the Capital during the plague of 1736 disposed the Church to look less coldly upon this unorthodox saint; and the ecclesiastics even began to hold some perfunctory ceremonies in her honor. Indeed, Maximilian, in his desire to conciliate the Mexicans, walked barefooted along the dusty road from the Capital to the shrine of Guadalupe, a distance of two miles and a half. In the imperial hands were lighted candles, and the imperial knees touched the ground before every wayside shrine along the route.

The Virgin of Guadalupe, like the Virgin of Los Remedios, is in politics. When the soldier-priest, Hidalgo, struck the first blow for Mexican independence he snatched from the altar of a neighboring church the banner of Guadalupe and unfurled it as the standard of Mexico. "Guadalupe, Guadalupe," was the war-cry of the Indians as they hurled themselves against the power of Spain, and it is small wonder that the name Guadalupe has hardly a saintly sound to churchly ears; nor need we marvel that the answering cry, "Remedios, Remedios," did not commend the Spanish saint to the Mexican patriot.

The standard of Mexico bears upon one side the figure of the Virgin of Guadalupe clothed in a long blue mantle. The halo encircles not merely the head, but the whole figure, giving it a resemblance to the Virgin of the Shell. On the reverse side of the standard is the eagle with the serpent in its claws. It is a curious fact that the three great republics of the world—France, Mexico

MEXICAN VISTAS 131

and the United States—have, or at some time have had, the eagle for a national emblem. The remembrance of this fact may well warm the heart of that proud bird.

The road to Guadalupe lies along the great northern causeway from the Capital. The route is

HOLY STAIRWAY, GUADALUPE.

bordered with shrines which have been erected by the pilgrims, and has quite the air of a Mexican Appian Way. We descended from the street car in the market place of the village, and were immediately captured by beggars. Mexican beggars, as a rule, are not persistent, but these boys yelled and hooted, and stood in our way, insisting upon leading us in every direction we did not wish to go and showing us all the sights we did not care to see, all the time demanding in terrific voices, "Centavos, centavos!" Finding we could not shake them off, we went our leisurely way pretending to be unconscious of their presence.

There is a little chapel built over a spring which gushed from the print of the Virgin's foot, where it is proper to drink from the mug which is offered irrespectively to all comers. It is a chalybeate spring, which may account for the doubtful odor of the water, which is hardly the odor of sanctity. Nevertheless, I believe some remarkable cures have been wrought by it.

We climbed the long flight of stairs to the chapel on the hill, the scene, according to tradition, of the Virgin's first appearance, passing on the way the curious Stone Sails of Guadalupe. No one knows the true story of these, but they are doubtless the thank-offering of some pious sailor. The chapel on the hill is the entrance to a pretty, carefully tended cemetery. Half way down the hill is the pathetic little grotto of the Virgin, which has been decorated by the Indian women of the village with bits of colored glass, silvered paper and pebbles. The fourth and largest church, at the foot of the hill, formerly contained the sacred tilma of Juan-Diego, but we learned on inquiry that the relic had been removed to the grand new Cathedral near by, where we found it serving as an altarpiece. The tilma, which still retains the image of Our Lady of Guadalupe, is of coarse fabric, but the color is bright and fresh and the figure of the Virgin as distinct as when new. It is said that many "distinguished scientists" have examined the tilma and are unable to explain the phenomenon. At all events Mexican theologians are doubly blessed, for they have the liberty of choosing between the wooden Virgin of Los Remedios and the cloth Virgin of Guadalupe.

The new Cathedral of Guadalupe, built specially for the preservation of the tilma, has already cost more than $2,000,000. It is decorated with huge paintings, the offerings of the different cities of Mexico. The interior of the church, which is not so overloaded with gilding as most of the other Mexican churches, is really beautiful; some of the stained glass is fine, and there is in front of the altar a good statue in marble of one of the former bishops. In the market place outside the church there are numberless booths for the sale of immensely long candles, and although the people look too poor to buy bread there are always plenty of purchasers. As we sat in the church a number of

134   MEXICAN VISTAS

penitents, carrying lighted candles several feet long in each hand, crawled from the entrance door to the high altar, upon their knees. There was about these poor souls an air of proud proprietorship in their favorite saint, and I could not find it in my heart to criticise their mental or spiritual attitude. Doubtless superstition is as great an inspiration to them as enlightened religion is to us, and no one who knows how utterly empty these patient lives are would wish to deprive them of any hope for the present or the future.

STONE SAILS.

TRAIL IN THE BARRANCAS—*page 117.*

CHAPTER XIV.

If we take at the Plaza the mule-car marked Atzcapotzalco—please pronounce slowly and distinctly—and follow the route along the main causeway, past Alvarado's Leap, the Church of the Martyrs, the Pantheon, and the little Church of San Cosme (upon the steeple of which the young Lieutenant, U. S. Grant, during the siege of Mexico planted a cannon), we will come to the Garita Gate. Just beyond this gate is Popotla, formerly a great broom market, now famed for the "tree of noche triste," under whose spreading branches Cortés sat down that fateful night and wept. The tree is in its decadence. Tradition has it that an infuriated Spaniard-hater once upon a time attempted to burn it, but the "higher criticism" of modern history insists that the tree was burned by a party of tourists who had the irreverence to boil their tea kettle in the sacred trunk. At all events the tree is badly scorched, and so mutilated by relic-hunters that the government has found it necessary to protect it by a high iron railing. Just beyond Popotla is the old town of Tlacopan, now called Tacuba, the residence of the Archbishop of Mexico.

A short ride brings us to Atzcapotzalco, which was, in the days of Montezuma, the quarters of the famous goldsmiths, whose cunning work so enchanted the Spaniards. It was also the Aztec slave market, where the captives taken in war who were not reserved for sacrifice were made profitable merchandise. The present inhabitants of Atzcapotzalco have still the air of being slaves—only they buy and sell their master, the tyrant pulque. It is amusing to sit in the plaza and watch the people in the market place selling fruit, vegetables, cotton cloth, flowers, and pottery. The word Atzcapotzalco signifies "ant hill," and one is struck by the ant-like efforts, in the wrong direction, of many of these poor people. Sometimes the little zocalo is a veritable battle-ground. We saw one day a tall, fine-looking policeman dragging a drunken man to jail. The officer was followed by a horde of howling women who trod on his heels, stood in his path, and ever and anon snatched his prisoner from him. But not the slightest change passed over the policeman's face. He only seized the prisoner more firmly in his grasp, and with the air of brushing away annoying insects, held on his course, and the whole struggling, vituperating, rabble at last disappeared under the arch of the prison door. Near Atzcapotzalco is the spring in which Guatemotzin is supposed to have hidden his treasure from the rapacity of the Spaniards. Over the buried treasure the spirit of the Indian maiden Marina is said still to stand guard. This patient spirit divides her time, spending part of the day at Chapultepec and part at Atzcapotzalco. Poor Marina is decidedly an overworked ghost.

Atzcapotzalco is the terminus of the street-car line from the City of Mexico. Another line to Tlanepantla starts from the plaza and if the traveler does not object to dust—which, however, is not excessive for Mexico—he will find the ride to that quaint little city an enchanting one. Along the road there are curious moldy churches, crumbling walls, old monasteries and convents, orchards of strange fruits, and, stretching far and wide, great fields of maguey. If pulque is good anywhere it is good at Tlanepantla; in fact, we liked the Tlanepantla brand better even than the far-famed brand of Apam. Tlanepantla is noted for its bull-fights, which are said to be festivals of merriment, rather than festivals of murder, and for the sake of the tortured animals of the country I hope the report is true. The oldest church in the town was built in 1583. The view of the volcanoes from the ancient city—especially in the afternoon—is one of the finest effects in the valley of Mexico.

As we entered the house of a friend in Tlanepantla one day, we found the sunny court filled with fettered men and armed soldiers. Our consternation was great, and we expected to see our friends brought out immediately for execution on the charge of high treason. Our hostess explained, however, that it was merely the chain-gang delivering wood bought that day at the market. What a field of speculation such a system of marketing opens up, to be sure. The delivery of butter by brigands, of poultry by parricides, and of furniture by felons must be a thrilling experience.

Another interesting trip is by horse-car from the City of Mexico to Tacubaya. Tacubaya lies on high ground, and during the great flood—which lasted from 1629 to 1634—it was decided to move the Capital thither, but when the flood subsided the plan was unfortunately abandoned. Tacubaya is more like one of our suburban towns than most suburban towns in Mexico, and there are in the quiet city really handsome houses, and gardens that answer to the exalted American idea of them. The city is called the Monte Carlo of Mexico, but we saw no gambling—perhaps because we did not know where to look for it. At all events the play is not so public as in other Mexican towns, where it is constantly before the eyes of the blindest innocence.

At Tacubaya we were astonished to see the energetic car-mules whisked off, and their place filled by a dummy engine which carried us over to Mixcoac, and thence to San Angel. We had on the road another beautiful picture of the valley of Mexico, which is certainly a basinful of fairy land. Mixcoac is a market-garden town and fruit and flowers are plenty and cheap. We strolled around San Angel and sat for awhile in the little plaza. A school for *ninas* (young girls) was in an old convent building near us, and we talked some time with the pupils, who were having recess in the wide corridors. These Mexican girls were very modest and pretty, and needed only a few exercises in physical culture to be charming. San Angel is another residence town for rich people doing business in the city. It has an old church, the interior of which was scaffolded to the dome for regilding, repairs, and frescoing. The barber-shop style of decoration will soon ruin all these fine old Mexican churches.

The San Mateo horse-car line takes us to the town of Coyacan, whither, after the capture of the Capital, Cortés and his captains retired to celebrate their victory. These martial missionaries and original expansionists were not too godly to turn their banquet into a drinking bout so scandalous that the good priest and confessor of the army not only put them under rigid penance, but afterward preached a sermon denouncing their misdeeds. In Coyacan Cortés lived with Marina while rebuilding

CORTES' PALACE, COYACAN.

the City of Mexico, and here, in a little garden attached to his house, he is said to have drowned his wife, who to his displeasure had followed his rising sun to Mexico from her humble home in Cuba. Tradition has it that her body lies over yonder in the little graveyard. Prescott, however, defends Cortés from this accusation of murder, explaining that "the high altitude made the climate very unhealthy for Donna Catalina, so that she died in three months after her arrival in the country, an event very much to the advantage of Cortés." Doubtless "high altitude" had a hand in the poor Donna's taking off, for she was of humble birth and tastes, and the Conqueror desired a noble wife. Still, I am inclined to believe that a busy man like

Cortés did not spend his life in wife-murder, as the guide-books would have us believe.

A short distance from San Angel, near San Mateo, is the battlefield of Cherubusco, where there is an old church and monastery. In the church are some very curious wooden figures of the patron and patroness, Don Diego del Castillo, and Donna Helena de la Cruz. In front of the monastery is a monument to the Mexicans who fell in the battle. Three weeks after the battle of Cherubusco the Americans, marching on to Chapultepec, gained the victories of Casa Mata, and Molino del Rey. Upon the capture of the powder magazine, from which the latter place takes it name, the young Lieutenant, U. S. Grant, was the first to enter the fort. Five days later the army scaled the heights of Chapultepec, which seemingly a dozen men might have held in the face of a much more numerous foe, and the City of Mexico lay in the hollow of their hand.

There are so many interesting pilgrimages in Mexico that a tourist should really take his household belongings—above all, his cook—camp in a town until the neighboring country has been explored, and then move on. As most of us, however, have limitations, both of time and money, it is well to choose the places to visit. An interesting town is Tlalpam, the former capital of the State of Mexico. It is a flower town, but it has also cotton, woolen, and paper mills. Long ago Whitsuntide gambling fête was yearly held here, which became so outrageous that the government suppressed it.

Texcoco is another ancient Aztec city whose inhabitants, together with the Tlascalans, became allies of the Spaniards and thus made the Mexicans slaves of the Castilians. This town, from which Cortés launched the brigantines with which he captured the City of Mexico, was the royal residence of that poet, warrior, and prince, the great Nezahualcoytl, who built a temple to the "Unknown God, the Cause of Causes." No image was allowed in this temple, and its altars were never stained with human sacrifice; the only offerings were of flowers, gums, and sweet spices. The son and successor of Nezahualcoytl was Nezahualpilli, a man of Roman virtues and austerities. Nezhaulpilli's son fell in love with a lady of the court, the Lady of Tula, with whom he carried on a poetical correspondence, which the historian says was a capital offense. We are left in the dark as to whether the crime lay in the existence of the correspondence, or whether the offense was in the fact that the correspondence was in verse. At all events the unfortunate prince paid for the indiscretion with his life. Although the king steeled his heart against the voice of nature, and allowed the cruel sentence to be carried out, he shut himself up in his own palace for months, and commanded the windows of his son's rooms to be walled up so that no one might ever again look from them. This stern monarch, severe in all things, once put to death a judge for taking a bribe, and a magistrate for deciding a suit in his own house.

In the days of the great Nezahualcoytl a league was formed between the three powers—Texcoco, Mexico, and the little kingdom of Tlacopan. In this coalition Texcoco may be said to have played the part of Athens, Mexico of Rome, while Tlacopan was the silent and humble member. The Texcocan prince was naturally, by the dignity of his character as well as by the superiority of his code of laws and general government, the head of the league. But at the time of the coming of Cortés the Aztec prince, Montezuma, had extended his power and possessions to the decided disadvantage of his neighbor, whose territory he had seized, and whose supremacy he had arrogated to himself. Nezahualpilli, depressed and humbled by the aggressions of his faithless colleague, soon died, and a contest between his two sons for the throne ensued. The claims of the elder were supported by Montezuma, who by this decision incurred the hatred of the younger son Ixtlilxochitl, a hatred which caused the young prince to declare himself an ally of the Spaniard.

As before stated, it was from Texcoco that Cortés

GARDENS OF LA BORDA, CUERNAVACA.

started on his second and successful expedition against the City of Mexico. Here too he dwelt for a season, when in disgrace with his Spanish sovereign, and here, for a time, his bones lay buried.

The Texcoco of the present day is a pretty little town with a plaza containing some statuary, the "laughing hill"—a favorite resort of Nezahualcoytl, and a stone basin called "Montezuma's Bath."

CHAPTER XV.

The hot morning we left Mexico for Cuernavaca we were delighted to find ourselves in a clean, bright, American car, which from comparison with the Mexican cars seemed a veritable palace. Of course in this criticism of the Mexican coaches I do not include those of the through trains north of the City of Mexico, which all carry Pullman cars.

The line to Cuernavaca—"the battle route"— passes the fields of Casa Mata, Molino del Rey, Padierna—where there is a monument to the United States' soldiers—and Contreras, while within a short distance can be seen the field of Cherubusco. After leaving Contreras the road constantly climbs, giving at every turn magnificent views of the valley of Mexico, with its seven shining lakes, its white volcanoes, its castle-crowned hill of Chapultepec, and the green villages dotting the plain. The route passes for a long distance through the desolate lava waste of the extinct volcano Ajusco—thrown up in an eruption sometime during the last century—and at El Guarda, an old outpost, the elevation is 10,000 feet above the sea. Just beyond La Cima—the highest point on the route—the road begins to descend, and soon after we pass the Cross of the Marquis, the ancient boundary of Cortés' grant in this valley. The forest of Huitzilac was, a generation ago, the favorite haunt of brigands.

For nearly two hours before reaching Cuernavaca the city lies at the traveler's feet, every turn upon the mountain side bringing him a little nearer to the enchanted land. From the vegetation of the temperate zone we look down on a little bit of tropical still life, and we realize the marvels of the Mexican climate which piles the temperature and the products of one zone upon those of another. It is well to remember that it is better to visit Cuernavaca early in the season, for we found the March weather in that delightful city a little oppressive. It is only fair to add, however, that we met there invalids who did not agree with us, but who found in the altitude of 5,000 feet and the dry warm air a cure for their ills. The town is picturesquely situated on a tongue of high land, cut on each side by deep barrancas or cañons. From these barrancas the country slopes gently down to the hot coast lands.

The people who live in Cuernavaca are never weary of sounding its praises. Said an American resident to me: "I lived in California; I froze in winter and roasted in summer. I tried Florida, and the fleas devoured me alive; here in Cuerna-

LAKE IN GARDENS OF LA BORDA.

vaca a flea is unknown." As about a dozen fleas were at that very moment lunching upon my person I did not accept her statement with the enthusiasm she expected. Nevertheless I am too old a traveler to be prejudiced by such little discrepancies, and am willing to admit that Cuernavaca is in most respects ideal, and that the water is beyond criticism.

The gardens of La Borda are a delightful retreat from the heat of the morning hours. These gardens, which were laid out in the last century by Joseph La Borda, a Frenchman who made a fortune in the silver mines, cost a million dollars. They are an imitation of the stiff architectural style of the gardens of Versailles, but the lavish tropical vegetation does its best to drape and soften the harsher features. There are stretches of cement walks bordered with vases of blooming plants, stone balustrades overhung with tropical fruits and flowers, and artificial lakes with wide sweeping steps leading down to the brink. Here in these fragrant aisles the proud and passionate Carlotta ate out her heart in solitude, while Maximilian dallied with a Mexican mistress in his pretty summer house three miles away. To the average woman, and, I sincerely hope, to the average man, what a conundrum is Maximilian. He could die like a hero, but he could not live a pure and loyal life; he could give up existence for what he called his "faith," but he could not give up one ignoble desire for the fond heart which his misfortunes drove to madness.

In Cuernavaca is the old palace of Cortés, still the handsomest building in town. Here, under the title of Marquis of the Valley, the Conqueror, when disgusted with his treatment by the Audience, retired, and spent a few quiet years in the cultivation of his vast estates. He introduced from Cuba the sugar-cane, and gave his attention to sheep-raising and the cultivation of the silk-worm. In one of the rooms of the palace Cortés is said to have murdered a wife; although he had several Indian mistresses he had only two wives, and the second one outlived him. In regard to this accusation, therefore, I think we must bring in the verdict not guilty. In this palace lived the beloved second wife of Cortés, the beautiful Donna Juana, to whom he gave as a marriage gift the five finest emeralds in the world. It was an unfortunate gift for the ardent lover, for the queen of Charles V. coveted the jewels, and the imprudent marriage-offering doubtless affected the later fortunes of the Great Captain. Poor Donna Juana had an anxious and lonely time of it during the long absences of her restless mate, and it was with a sad heart that she saw him embark with her little son for his last disastrous voyage to Spain. Cortés, like Columbus, was fated to know the bitterness of unappreciated services. Charles V. refused to give audience to his complaint, and the proud old man was driven to supplications most touching from one of Cortés' character. "Who is that?" queried the Emperor on one occasion when Cortés endeavored to press into his presence. "One who has given you more kingdoms than you had towns before," was the stern reply. After seven years of waiting upon the favor of a faithless monarch the broken-hearted old man died at Seville, and the Mexicans were avenged.

In front of the palace of Cortés is one of the most picturesque market places in Mexico. The little

MARKET PLACE, CUERNAVACA.

zocalo at the sides of the palace entrance has a velvety sward, and realizes the American idea of a park. The pansies grown there are the largest I have ever seen. Immediately in front of the palace is the statue of one of the former governors of the

State—a keen-eyed, war-visaged, one-armed soldier. Water is abundant in Cuernavaca, and the tinkle of the falling streams is heard along the streets bordered by high walls which conceal the dense growth of tropical orchards.

The evenings at Cuernavaca are magical. As the twilight gathers, the Mexicans, like the Jews, seek the housetop. There, on the flat roof, under the shadow of the grim Cathedral bearing in its tower the old clock presented by Charles V. to Cortés, and looking down upon the narrow streets where the great Captain and his cavaliers had so often ridden on their ruthless way, we saw the sun go down. We saw the light die on the breast of the "sleeping woman," Ixtaccihuatl, and the red flush fade slowly from the cheek of her watching lover, Popocatapetl. Then the western sky broke up into drifting fleeces of crimson and gold, the fires of the charcoal burners blinked from the hillsides, the deep bell boomed from the Cathedral tower, the voices of the street, the bleat of the goats and the tinkle of the cow bells came faintly through the soft air, and all at once we were up, up, up, at the foot of the stars. From these enchanted heights the white-jacketed mozo recalled us, and in a languid dream we descended the long flights of stairs, crossed the dim, flower-scented court, and ate our frugal supper by the light of a smoky kerosene lamp.

There are beautiful rides around Cuernavaca and the services of a confidential and congenial little donkey can be procured for a small sum. There are also, for those who do not mind rough roads, picturesque drives of a few miles to waterfalls, caves, lakes and ruined temples. The delights of the landscape are inexhaustible. Add to this an almost perfect winter climate, an altitude not too high for active exercise, and comfortable hotels—the Alarcon is an American house—and you have all the things essential to the comfort and happiness of a traveler.

CHAPTER XVI.

"Early to bed and early to rise," is the motto of the Mexican railroads, whose trains start out at daybreak and stop for the night. As if the early wakening were not discomfort enough, no hotel or restaurant in any city furnishes breakfast for the departing traveler.

Innocently unconscious of this eccentricity on the part of Mexican landlords, we wandered one morning, in the half-light, through the streets of the Capital seeking our matutinal meal. The Iturbide, the Sanz, the Jardin and the French and American restaurants presented to us closed doors and darkened windows. A policeman, carrying a dying lantern, to whom we at last appealed, told us that we would find breakfast at the *estacion;* so calling an early rising, shabby, yellow-flag cab, we hastened thither. We found outside of the station a group of tables covered with coffee-stained towels, and surrounded by a motly throng of shabby Spaniards, Mexicans in dirty serapes, Indians,

dark-faced women with their babies hanging to their backs, and pert dandies in golden spurs and velvet jackets. Eggs and coffee were cooking over a smoking brazier of burning charcoal, whose feeble glow was kept alive by the energetic use of a fan of cactus fiber. We ate our sour bread and drank our inky coffee with humble and contrite hearts, for our meal was made a most mournful one by the supplications of a pack of half-starved dogs who eyed each crumb wistfully.

The Mexican R. R., or "Queen's Own," was built and is controlled by an English company. The first-class cars, which are poorly ventilated and uncomfortable, were crowded with commercial travelers. As usual I was the only woman. The Mexican women do not travel, and no arrangement for the comfort of the señoras is made on the railway trains or in the hotels. Our poor sisters must have a very dull life. They are expected to go to church and pray for their husbands who will not pray for themselves, take care of the countless babies of the household, and keep their faces properly powdered. As a reward of merit they are occasionally treated to a street-car ride, but the idea of public duties or public life in any form for women, fills our neighbors with horror. Fortunately the men are generous and chivalric and are always ready to toil for their female relations.

The Mexican R. R., one of the scenic routes of the country, owing to the difficulties of construction and operation, is, perhaps, the costliest in the world. It may be said to be a holy railroad, as it was commenced under the auspices of the Church, and before making its first trip received the solemn blessing of the ecclesiastical dignitaries. As we leave the city behind us, the churches and sacred shrine of Guadalupe come into view. Then from the plain arise the Pyramids of the Sun and the Moon at San Juan Teotihuacan, the former of which is more than half the size of the great Pyramid of Cheops in Egypt. Between the two pyramids the Street of the Dead can be distinctly traced from the flying train. Otumba, several miles further on, was Cortés' battleground, a few days after the defeat of "Noche Triste." We soon enter the maguey country, and if we drink pulque at all, it is well to drink it at Apam, where the pulque is considered the best in Mexico. If we are sufficiently recovered from the dose by the time we reach Apizaco, it is our duty as orthodox tourists to descend from the train and buy canes. At Apizaco we had an experience which contradicted—as many of our experiences did—the assertions of those Americans who contend that the Mexicans are all dishonest. A Mexican commercial traveler, a courteous and intelligent man, offered his advice on the subject of canes, and rebuked the vender for selling them of unseasoned wood, which is liable to warp and change color. This sale of unseasoned wood is, by the way, as we afterward discovered, a common fraud in dealing with tourists. Our Mexican friend, although himself a resident of the city, also had the honesty to advise us not to stay any time in Vera Cruz, as he knew of several cases of yellow fever in the town; and this, too, in spite of the fact that the railroads and hotels were constantly asserting that Vera Cruz was entirely free from the scourge.

After leaving Apizaco the road skirts the base of the volcano Malintzi, while on the other hand rises Orizaba, his head buried in the clouds. Here is a stretch of country that is a veritable desert. The dust powders everything, and choking, perspiring humanity sees no beauty in Mexico. At Esperanza we slipped over the edge of the high plateau down into the chasm, dropping 4,000 feet in about thirty miles. The rush down grade, with brakes set, from the temperate to the torrid zone, was exciting. As we whirled, rocking around curve after curve, we looked down into deep, garden-like valleys, and up mountain slopes covered with blue and white ageratum, scarlet mimulus, gorgeous crimson tulips, and countless tropical blossoms unknown to us. We saw at last the little town of Maltrata, its red-tiled roofs shining in the sun 2,000 feet below us, and when, after a long detour, we steamed into the pretty station, we found women selling, in a really tropical climate, strange tropical fruits and orchids. To our amazement we also recognized the same Indian peddlers who had besieged us at our last stopping place on the mountain side. These unregenerate sons of the soil had taken the short cut, and while we were writhing and twisting around the curves they had rolled comfortably down the slope and were at the foot ready to greet us, as noisy and as aggressive as ever.

After leaving Maltrata we entered the cañon of the Infernillo—little hell. The stream that rushes through the cañon accompanied us down into the green valley, and thence to Orizaba, where it sang all night under our windows lulling us to happy sleep. There are two hotels in Orizaba, the Diligencias and La Borda—both of them good. We chose the latter one, and were rewarded by a little bit of French life, which, after so much of Mexico, was charming. We ate our well-cooked dinner of potage, poulet, salade jardiniere, and wholesome vin ordinaire, with thankful hearts. We intended to drink a gallon of the tempting water, but were immediately warned that the last guests had been made very ill by it, so that we were obliged to content ourselves with the song of the brook under our windows and the dash of the blessed rain against the pane. After the high, dry air and the choking dust of the plateau we reveled in the soft, damp, atmosphere of the lower levels.

The great industries of Orizaba are the cotton factories—situated in the green valley in the neighborhood of Nogales—the sugar mills and the coffee plantations. The cotton mills, like those of Querétaro, although in a climate peculiarly adapted to raising cotton, obtain most of their supply from New Orleans. These mills, which are very extensive, are equipped with modern machinery, and have altogether a most un-Mexican nineteenth century air. We visited one of the sugar houses and saw the cane crushed, pressed into syrup, and then boiled and strained. The finished product is very sweet and pure, but the dark-colored cakes weighing several pounds each are not tempting. Behind the sugar house that we visited is a beautiful garden with a gorgeous display of hibiscus.

Orizaba is one of the great coffee centers of Mexico. The coffee plant, with its smooth, shining leaves, and red berries, somewhat resembles a dwarf cherry. The red fruit, when split, is found to contain two coffee berries lying face to face. As the common belief is that the coffee plant suffers from the direct rays of the sun, it is generally grown under the shadow of a banana or some other fruit tree. Nevertheless a successful coffee grower assured us that such a shield is unnecessary, as he had raised the finest coffee without any covering. So it seems that the rules governing coffee culture are like those governing politics and religion—every man chooses his own. In Orizaba the coffee grows in an orthodox fashion under the banana. These broad-leaved plants, with their great clusters of fruit ending in the huge swinging tassel of the purple blossoms, attain a height of twelve or fifteen feet.

The drive to the Four Cascades is along a pleasant road leading through a plantation, between the pale green files of the waving cane fields and the shining coffee plants. A pretty little dark-faced elf of a child came running from one of the cane-walled, palm-thatched huts to beg of us, and then, half-frightened at our strange faces, ran back again to the sheltering arms of her liquid-eyed mother. The pair would have delighted the pencil of a Murillo. All along the wayside grew bright-hued flowers; the scarlet honeysuckle tangled the grasses and the Four Cascades were literally set in blossoms. We were told, to our disgust, that the power in these waterfalls was to be utilized for manufacturing, and that the beauty of the spot was to be destroyed.

As we turned to leave the Cascades we saw on

the ground what looked to be a moving mat of verdure, which upon investigation proved to be composed of small leaves about the size of watercress leaves. Each little leaf was borne upon the back of an agile ant. There was an army of these little insects, all in active motion, seemingly with some point in view. It was evident that the apathy of the climate had not crept into the veins of this army with the green banners. In view of the destruction of the waterfalls we at first expressed a wish that the industries of mankind could be carried on with as little injury to the beauties of nature as the industries of these tiny earth-toilers. But as, upon closer examination, these busy ants seemed to us to resemble the bebehanas of Cuba, which dismantle an orchard in a few hours, we concluded to be satisfied with the destructive abilities of our kind.

There is the usual equipment of churches in Orizaba, several of which contain creditable pictures by a local artist, Gabriel Barranca, who seems to draw his inspiration from the old masters. Naturally, however, his isolated life imposes upon him serious limitations. There is a good monument in the pretty plaza, and over on the hill is a cross which marks one of the battle grounds of the French invasion. The city is, on the whole, a charming place, but to us, after the dry, treeless, plains of central Mexico, the most glorious things in Orizaba were "God's first temples," and his blessed rain.

CHAPTER XVII.

We reluctantly left Hotel La Borda in the dimness of an early ,morning and were bounced through the muddy streets of Orizaba to the station. The route between Orizaba and Vera Cruz is even more picturesque than between Esperanza and Orizaba. The Barranca or Cañon of the Metlac, with its leaping river 1,000 feet below the rails, and its moist, tropical vegetation, is one of the finest bits of scenery on the Mexican railways. The road leads on, always descending, through jungle-like forests and fields of gorgeous bloom to the curious old town of Cordova. Cordova was formerly a very important place, but as white men find the unhealthy climate unfitted for labor the town has, since the emancipation of the slaves, declined greatly in importance. The quaint streets of the old city have a foreign and almost a ghoulish air, but it is in Cordova that one sees the tropical fruits in their fullest perfection. Here we were served with the only real pineapples I ever ate out of Cuba. I will not go so far as to say that they equaled the creamy Cuban pineapple, but they were not in the least like those hard cones, seemingly soaked in sulphuric acid, which we of the north call pineapples. Of course travelers in Cordova are, sooner or later, inveigled into buying one of those immense bushel basket bouquets of scarlet or white camelias which are sold on the street for about ten cents of our money.

After leaving Cordova we slid off from the last of the mountain benches into the tierra caliente, or tropical lands near the coast. The ride through the dank jungles and over the dazzling reaches of white sand to Vera Cruz is a hot one, and the end of it all is discomfort and extortion. Our experience in Vera Cruz was that of most travelers. The birds of prey—not the feathered ones, which fortunately we escaped—picked our bones. The street-car line, which is owned by the state, allows no carriages in the city. In addition to this sin against the traveling public the company seems to be also in league with the *cargadores*, or porters, and no car meets the trains; so the tourist, fresh from a cool climate, is obliged to walk through the noon-day heat of a tropical sun to the hotel. I headed the perspiring and eloquent procession, bearing a huge white bouquet of Cordova camelias, which gave me the appearance of a bride carrying my wedding cake to the church. The camelias bore the ordeal better that I did, for I think I should surely have fainted had not three big turkey buzzards followed me with hungry eyes, and I was afraid to fall lest they should pick me up.

Cortés landed at Vera Cruz, just south of the Island of San Juan de Alloa. Upon the sandy beach of that most beautiful of all seas, the Gulf of Mexico, he established his camp and planted his artillery. His little army suffered fearfully from the heat of the spring sun—it was in the month of April—and the swamps and marshes in the vicinity pouring out their deadly exhalations soon brought the now-dreaded *vomito* or yellow fever, until that time practically unknown. Undeterred, however, by the heat, by pestilence, by venomous insects, the terrors of a savage foe, or the dangers of a strange country, the conquerors built the town, which they called Villa Rica de Vera Cruz—the Rich City of the True Cross. In August the army quitted the new town and moved forward across the beautiful lands of the *tierra caliente* and up the mountain sides to the table lands of central Mexico. Three hundred and twenty-five years later General Scott landed on the same spot, and from the City of Vera Cruz started on his victorious march to the City of Mexico.

There is little to see in Vera Cruz except the

dirty streets, the turkey buzzards, which act as general garbage commissioners, and a horrible black figure of Christ, which blemishes one of the churches. The Vera Cruzans dwell with ecstasy upon the fact that there is only one other like it in the world. I should hope not. The other one, which is in Havana, is fully as ugly as that in Mexico, and neither of them has any spiritual significance. The town of Vera Cruz has every reason to be the unhealthiest place in the world, for, in addition to the deadly climate, the sewage runs in open gutters by the side of the street, and the pedestrian and the burro alike stir up the living mass. To add to the other discomforts, numerous energetic insects abound which eat everything, even to wood, so that the telegraph and telephone poles are made of iron.

For the foregoing, and a few other reasons, we were only too glad to turn our backs on Vera Cruz, where everybody, from the waiter to the express company, swindled us, and join the triumphal procession on its march to the station. I will add, for the benefit of future travelers, that it is best not to take heavy baggage to Vera Cruz, for the railroad charges enormously for the smallest trunks, and that if you trust your hand-baggage to a *cargadore* it is better to have the contract with him as to price sworn to before a public notary. We neglected

this wise precaution, and were obliged to pay just four times the tariff demanded for such service in the City of Mexico. It is useless to appeal to the authorities, for they are all in league with whatever enterprise puts a little unlawful money into the purse of the Vera Cruzans. It was therefore with a feeling of exultation that we at last got off, and from all accounts got off cheaply, from the Rich City of the True Cross. The fresh sea breeze blew through the car, and swept from our garments and from our minds all bitter thoughts of Vera Cruz, its intolerable odors, its yellow fever, and its birds of prey. After all, this was the only unpleasant, if not the only uncomfortable, experience we had in Mexico.

The country between Vera Cruz and Jalapa, where the train stops for the night, is rich and capable of a high cultivation. In these fertile wastes are hidden mines of gold waiting to be dug out by a race with the energy for the work and the physique to endure the climate. The International R. R., a narrow-gauge road, is in some places a marvelous piece of engineering. Within a distance of a few miles there are nearly one hundred horse-shoe curves, and at Harumbo, the deepest railway cut in Mexico, there is a complete loop. Just before reaching Jalapa we crossed the battlefields of Cerro Gordo, and National Bridge, where Scott won notable victories in the Mexican war. Soon after crossing the bridge we saw a glow ahead of us, and out of the darkness and the rain we rolled into the electric-lighted station of Jalapa.

Jalapa is remarkable for several things. To the weary traveler the most important of its many advantages is the fact that it has one of the best hotels in Mexico, with electric lights and a court filled with tropical bloom. If I mention also the fact that the breakfast table is spread with brown oil-cloth and that only tearful supplications will move the stony-hearted mozo to indulge the breakfaster with a plate, it is not in a spirit of carping criticism, but merely to remind myself that even a sugar-coated pill has a bitter heart, and that life—especially in Mexico—is full of vicissitudes.

Jalapa was an old town even in Cortés' day, and since his invading army marched through its narrow streets many other armies have come and gone. The Americans, after the battle of Cerro Gordo—which was fought on that round-topped hill over yonder—and the battle of National Bridge, marched through Jalapa, and in their victorious ranks marched Grant and Thomas, Longstreet and Lee. Down these streets went also a retreating army led by Marshal Bazaine, the great French Retreater, who, afterward, in the Franco-Prussian war, surrendered a force of 125,000 full-grown men;

Bazaine took the road to Vera Cruz, where he embarked with his troops for France, leaving poor Maximilian to his fate.

An important source of revenue to Jalapa is that old-fashioned drug, jalap. We hear little of it in this generation, but it doubtless enters into the composition of many of the patent "liver invigorators" of the present day. The bitter jalap is a near relation of our sweet climbing morning-glory, so we see that even the flower families have their unpleasant connections. The principal business of Jalapa seems to be gambling, and in the evening the little plaza is given over to the white tent and the white umbrella, under whose shade keno, monte and other games are extensively patronized. The government receives twenty per cent of the revenues, and in addition has a lottery of its own which yields immense profits. One day while we were in Jalapa an official drawing took place, and the winning numbers were posted in all the public places.

We went one afternoon, between the showers, to the neighboring village of Coatepec, where one sees the coffee haciendas of Mexico in their fullest perfection. The funny little tramway runs through a New England hill country, and a New England brook chatters beside the way. There is a pretty plaza and the usual church in Coatepec, but I could not fathom the secret of its attraction for bridal couples. Four happy pairs accompanied us on the trip and made Ahasuerus and myself feel like hard-hearted worldlings—without love and without ideals. It is evident that Mexican bridal couples, except for their richer tints, are much like American brides and bridegrooms.

There is a charming trip down a picturesque ravine to Jiltopec, which, if one appreciates scenery from the point of view of the back of a dripping burro, is well worth taking. The old town, too, with its torturing pavements of sharp cobblestones, its narrow streets washed clean by the rain, and its quaint overhanging roofs, is romantic enough to tempt the stranger to a long sojourn; but unhappily Jalapa is most of the time in the clouds and its skies continually do weep. It rained and rained, and after listening to the woeful tale of a commercial traveler who had been waiting in the hotel eighteen days for fair weather to take a mountain trip, we went our way. But fate was kind to us, for, the morning before we left, the skies cleared for a time, and we saw the beautiful mountain Orizaba rising before us like a white spirit. At the right, in the golden clefts of the burned-out volcano Perote, were heaped masses of fleecy clouds which overflowed and dripped down the mountain side in snowy garlands; but while we looked, holding our breaths lest we should lose something, the gray curtain dropped down again, and Orizaba and Perote became once more invisible to the eyes of moist but enraptured flesh.

CHAPTER XVIII.

I think the matter has not been before mentioned, but to me the Mexican commercial traveler seems to have round eyes of an owl-like sagacity and a voice that is almost a hoot. These peculiarities I credit to his living so much in the half-light. I am persuaded that if I should for two years catch the early trains and travel on the late ones I should develop circular visual organs, a coat of feathers and a desire to roost in a tree-top. The morning we left Jalapa we rose at four o'clock, and took our breakfast from the obnoxious oil tablecloth, decorated for the occasion with coffee and beer rings. We could not obtain from the flinty-souled mozo, even for a consideration, the boon of a plate—we were the parting guests and our nimble nickles were worth only their face value. We felt that our reign was indeed over, and sadly and humbly we gathered up the crumbs scattered over the brown oil-cloth and swallowed them with an abject spirit.

Mexican movements are slow. It seemed to us

that we got up to catch the train about bed time, but the sun was tinting the sky with salmon and gold when we finally steamed out of the station. For long hours we rode through the black ashes of the dead volcanic fires with which that great peak, the Coffre de Perote, has strewn these regions. There must have been troublous times here once, and one cannot help fearing that Mexico will sometime again see the fires kindled upon her mountain tops; but the shimmering mists are seemingly anxious to hide the desolation, and as we climbed upward

A MEXICAN HACIENDA.

the black waste was buried under blankets of fleecy clouds. Over this same mountain road, above these floating masses, and through these burned-out ashes, went Cortés before us; and we see his handiwork in the immense fortifications of the Castle of Perote, which was built to defend the highway over which the Spanish army, marching into the interior, received all its supplies.

As we slipped down the last range of mountains the valley, with its waving grain fields and the white towers of the far-off haciendas, came into view. At a distance these haciendas have really an air of elegance, and doubtless some of them are the homes of luxury and refinement; but generally it is best not to allow the nose to follow too closely after the eyes, and, above all, when in the immediate vicinity of many of these crowded plantations dismiss from your minds all preconceived prejudices on the subject of sanitation, cleanliness, or proper food. We visited one hacienda, the property of a man who had been many times governor of his state. It was a fine old place and had been in the family for more than three hundred years. From appearances I should judge that, in all that time, no water had touched the woodwork or the windows. The glass was festooned with dead flies, and the doors were so filthy that we would not touch them with our hands, but pushed them open with our feet. The meals, which were the worst we found in Mexico, were served by offensively unclean waiters, and the repasts were topped off by extract of coffee poured from an ancient, mildewed pepper-sauce bottle into a cup of dirty goat's milk.

But let us dismiss such ungracious remembrances from our minds, and remember only how beautiful, how like fairy palaces those fortress homes looked that sunny day, as they rose against the dusty horizon with the grandest of all the Mexican mountains—Malintzi—for a background. Malintzi bears upon its crest the great helmeted figure which to the superstitious Montezuma bore the likeness of the terrible stranger, Cortés. I saw distinctly the helmeted head and the massive limbs of the Conqueror, and then I read in the guidebook a vivid description of "the long hair of the maiden that streams down the mountain side." Evidently the writer did not see the same picture that we saw. What a beneficent providence it is that allows us to deck these profile mountains with the forms and the features that best please us.

Keeping always in sight of the four "smoking mountains"—Popocatepetl, Ixtaccihuatl, Orizaba and Malintzi—none of which, although native Mexicans, really smoke—we steamed across the plain toward the shining domes of Puebla. Puebla is a "holy city," founded by Cortés in the shadow of that other holy city, Cholulu, whose shrines he had despoiled, and whose innocent inhabitants he had put to the sword. According to tradition the town was laid out by angels, who, in their capacity of real-estate agents, gave all the corner lots to the church. Those who have visited Continental cities will agree that there seems to be a subtle relation between sanctity and smells, and that a holy city is apt to be rank to the nostrils. Puebla is no exception to the rule, although, as in the Capital, there is no visible reason for such a condition of affairs. The streets of the city look clean and the watering-pot and the cactus-fiber broom are everywhere in evidence. From the top of the hill of Cinco de Mayo the town, with its white walls and domes of shining tile, is really a dream city, and perhaps it is unkind to mention that there are other spots where Puebla seems to be another kind of a dream—a nightmare.

HOTEL CORRIDOR, PUEBLA

We could forgive Puebla everything, however, because of its salads. These salads are compounded of waxy white and green lettuce so daintily tinted that it feeds the eyes as well as the stomach. Upon the delicate greenery are piled little mounds of scarlet tomatoes and ivory slices of alligator pear, and over the whole is sprinkled, in exact proportions, a dressing of salt, pepper, and delicious oil. I never ate like salad elsewhere and I am inclined to believe that such gastronomic perfection is impossible except when mixed in a low, dark room clouded with tobacco smoke, and by a Mexican boy clad in a velvet jacket and with his hair dressed a la pompadour.

Puebla is highly esteemed of the guide-books for her tiled domes and buildings, which are certainly curious, much resembling the sample cards of the new spring styles of shirting. The city has been the battleground of Mexico. Here Iturbide, before he saw the star of liberty, met the army of Mexican patriots, and here General Scott's troops encamped after capturing the city. The hill of Cinco de Mayo is a historic mound. Up its rocky sides swarmed the French attacking the Mexicans, who, under General Zaragoza, had intrenched themselves in the little church of Guadalupe on the summit. The French army, at that time repulsed, was, four years later, besieged on the same hill and captured by General (now President) Diaz. At the foot of the hill is an equestrian statue of Zaragoza. It should have a companion one of Diaz, who not only fought for his country, but, like the good Juarez, has lived for her.

The great staple of Puebla is onyx. It is made into all sorts of useless and foolish articles which by no means tempt the purchaser. By the time an American has reached maturity, he is not inclined to throw away money on fat pears, diminutive flat-irons and absurd animals, even if made of the beautiful Puebla onyx. The Mexicans, however, thoroughly delight in childish toys, in beaded sombreros, tiny stirrups, gaudy dolls, and antique gods fresh from the factory. The markets of Puebla, like those of other Mexican towns, are delightful in the morning, and decidedly unappetizing later in the day. It was in the Puebla market that I first comprehended the real outwardness of tomales. I saw women gathering from the dirty floor the trodden cornhusks which had enveloped the tomales eaten in the market that day. These, we were told, were washed and served for another day. I ate no more tomales in Mexico.

As Puebla is a holy city, it is naturally filled with churches. The Cathedral is, in my opinion, much finer than the more famous one in the City of Mexico, although like the latter the beauty of the interior is marred by the choir in the middle of the nave. Still the size of the church prevents it from looking crowded, and the side altars are particularly fine. We were so unfortunate as to reach Puebla Easter week, and the constant clanging of the bells nightly broke our slumbers, for Puebla is sufficiently holy to defy civil law, which, for some reason, does not enforce its statutes against so-called church prerogatives. In spite, however, of the ecclesiastical atmosphere of the city, the sentiment of the people does not seem to me really religious. Indeed, the Holy Week services, with the clanging of meaningless bells, the high, dreary intonations of the priests, the swinging of the censers by irreverent boys, and the flashy music, seemed more like an auction than a religious service, and I could not help contrasting it with some most beautiful and impressive Holy Week services I once heard in the famous Cathedral of Amiens. Evidently the Mexicans have more pride in their national glory than love for, or belief in, their national religion. Neither have they that artistic sense which the Catholic Church has always delighted to foster. In the beautiful Church of the Soledad we were moved almost to tears at the sight of a bevy of workmen who were busily and contentedly covering the magnificent old gilded altars of the Chapel of the Rosary with shining white paint. The lovers of art on this continent should form a secret society for the purpose of stealing the paint pots from Mexico.

In the Church of San Francisco I found a new saint. I had already a patron saint—St. Barbara—who protects from all my individual terrors—thunder, lightning, gunpowder, and I hope also kerosene lamps. But she is a guardian saint, while my new one, who is called St. Sebastian de Aparicio, is a saint for imitation. He first introduced into Mexico oxen and wheeled carts, and for many years he drove the Cannon-Ball, Limited, Ox Express from Puebla to Vera Cruz. A series of pictures in one of the side chapels of the San Francisco represents the important events of his holy and useful life. In one picture we see him walking, dry-shod, over a river, while the heads of his swimming oxen are just visible above the surface of the water. In another picture angels are pulling the ox cart out of the mud. Heaven bless you, dear old work-a-day saint, and heaven bless your angels, for your creed of pious labor is the only one that will ever redeem this benighted land. You were the true apostle of civilization and enlightenment, the forerunner of the railways and the public schools. Let us hope that your saintly prayers will prevail upon those winged angels of the Lord, Knowledge and Industry, to come again, and pull this land out of the mire of sloth and ignorance.

We shall always remember Puebla on account of the remarkable adventures we had there while searching for baths. The guide-books speak with unction of the fine baths in the city, so we started out to find them. The first place we entered had good rooms, fine tubs and snowy towels—but ice-cold water. As we were already congealing in our furs, we did not care for that, so we drove in the teeth of a bitter wind at least two miles, to another part of the city, where there were said to be vapor baths. At the end of our Arctic expedition we were conducted by way of a miry cow-yard to a collection of dungeons, through whose grated floors ascended clouds of steam and incense which was not holy incense. The attendant said it was sulphur, but I fear it was a Mexican product, and not honest American sulphur. The maid also hazarded the opinion that the baths were good for all kinds of diseases, an assertion I did not question, for when I inhaled the steam I felt as though I had been exposed to yellow fever, smallpox and typhus, all at once; so with a shiver we wended our way back again through the cow-yard. I am glad to record that we did, in the end, find well-equipped baths in one of the hotels. I had a distinct impression, however, that the people of the place considered it highly indelicate for a señora to want a bath. It is a strange thing that in a climate where water is a necessity, and among conditions where only repeated and thorough soakings are effective, the bathtub is lacking in almost all homes and hotels, and the use of it is regarded, to say the least, as unusual and eccentric.

One autumn morning in the year 1519 the inhabitants of the sacred city of Cholulu rose early. For many days strange guests had tarried among them, whose marvelous fire-spitting weapons, awe-inspiring animals (horses were until that time unknown to the Mexicans), and personal prowess had kept the whole city in a state of terror. The time had now come when they were to be delivered from the presence of the feared and detested Spaniard, and the Cholulans, filled with joy at the prospect of their release, gathered in the plaza, under the shadow of the holy pyramid, upon whose summit the sacred fires were blazing. But in a moment this scene of joyful anticipation was turned into one of terror and anguish. Cortés and his army, affecting to doubt the faith of the people whose guests they had been, fell upon the gathered multitudes and put them all to the sword. The Indians, clad only in their cotton garments, offered little resistance to the sharp blades of the conquerors, whose heavy mail was proof against the light missiles of the Cholulans. Those who did not fall by the sword were mown down by the artillery or trampled under the feet of the horses, and the evening of the day that had opened so brightly saw smoking and blackened houses, and streets choked with dead bodies. The ruin of the city completed, Cortés ascended the pyramid to the teocalli, freed the victims awaiting sacrifice, burned the temple, and erected a cross in its stead. Thus in carnage and cruelty was inaugurated the first great missionary enterprise in America.

Cholulu, at the time of Cortés a very old city, must have been a holy place even before the coming of the Aztecs, for if the archeologists are right the

By Detroit Photo Co.

AGUADORS, CITY OF MEXICO—*page 27.*

pyramid was built not by the Cholulans, who were the contemporaries of the Aztecs, but by those great mound-builders, the Olmecs or Toltecs. Indeed, if we may believe Ignatius Donnelly, we may refer the hill to unknown antiquity; for this eccentric and enthusiastic investigator believes Cholulu to be the original Tower of Babel. The Aztec tradition credits the founding of the city to the god Quetzalcoatl, the greatest and best of all the Aztec divinities. It is related that Quetzalcoatl, fleeing from persecution, found an asylum among the Cholulans to whom he taught agriculture, weaving, architecture and the practical arts of peace. The mild creed of Quetzalcoatl was opposed to human sacrifice, and fruits and flowers were the offerings he taught the people to lay upon the altar. There is a legend among the southern Indians that the "bearded god," as the fair-skinned Quetzalcoatl was called, was in reality St. Thomas, who, fleeing from persecution, trusted himself to the unknown sea and landed on the coast of America. It is certain that the Spaniards did not first bring the Cross to Mexico, for one of the most amazing sights to the conquerors was the stone emblem which so often rose beside the teocalli. It was called by the natives the "Tree of Life," and its four arms pointing toward the cardinal points were supposed to be an appeal to the four winds of heaven to bring the wished-for rain.

The good and peaceful god Quetzalcoatl remained with the Cholulans for a season and then disappeared, promising to return again some time in the future. Although his flower-decked altars were soon desecrated with human sacrifice, the gentle god himself was not forgotten, and his second coming was looked for with much the same anticipations that the ancient Jews watched for the coming of the Messiah. It is not strange, therefore, that the superstitious Montezuma mistook the fair-skinned Cortés, with his bearded cavaliers, for the long looked-for god, and was not undeceived until too late to save his kingdom.

The mule-cars, which jolt along the rough road from Puebla to Cholulu, are comfortless and dirty; but the country through which they creak, with its reaches of waving grain, picturesque haciendas, and fields of maguey, is, when the dust lifts, really charming. As we climbed the long, winding way to the top of the pyramid, we saw the same landscape that Cortés, in his day, saw—the three volcanoes and the wind-swept plain. We saw also the shining domes of Puebla, that holy city founded by him in the place of the one he had so ruthlessly destroyed. The church which Cortés built on the site of the teocalli was destroyed by an earthquake, so that the chapel on top of the pyramid is, the location considered, more modern than one could wish, although its spiritual atmosphere seems positively archaic.

The modern Cholulan differs from his progenitor in one respect—he is not so anxious to speed the parting guest; rather is he desirous to bind him hand and foot, and keep him until his store of sheckles be exhausted. In exchange for the coveted silver he proposes to give bits of colored glass, small pebbles, idols with effaced features, and obsidian blades. But why should we judge harshly this poor offspring of a subject race. He has been so long himself a victim of robbery that it is little wonder that he has learned some of the lessons taught in the school of oppression.

The Cholulans are very poor, there is no doubt of it, and as we stood on the Pyramid, we saw the reason for this poverty. Rising above the valley, which has a population of about 5,000 souls, are the spires of twenty-seven churches—some of them in deserted fields distant from town and seemingly abandoned—a sad commentary upon the state of religion in Mexico. Evidently the new belief is not so vital as the faith it superseded, for in Cortés' day the temples were filled with worshipers, and here, upon this holy mount, the fires of the sacrifice were continually burning. Upon the pyramid of Cholulu alone twelve thousand victims were each year offered. The modern church has, however, only itself to blame for the present condition of affairs. It has wasted its revenues in needless church building, and puts its consolations,

ON THE STREETS OF CHOLULA.

even its holy sacraments, beyond the reach of any but a well-filled purse. We were constantly informed that marriage, on account of the attendant expense, was almost unknown among the poorer classes, and was unpopular among the middle classes. Indeed, a wise economy rules even so important a duty as the registration of births. A stringent ordinance was passed last winter requiring parents to register the births of all their children, and the Mexican public was treated to the amusing spectacle of fathers registering the births of grown-up and married children, and of young men themselves presenting their own birth certificates for record.

To study the modern Cholulan one should sit as we did in the sunny plaza, which is on the very spot where the ancient Cholulans were massacred, and gaze upon the loitering crowds. The markets, especially on Sunday morning, do a thriving business. The little piles of peas, beans, coffee, fruit and nuts, the tiny mounds of bacon, steaks and chops, the baskets of struggling, suffering poultry, and the squeaking pigs vainly tugging to free their legs from the cruel rope, are like those seen in all the Mexican market places. On the four sides of the plaza extend the churches, and under their holy shadow—but not always in accordance with their divine ordinances—the buying and the selling, the struggling and the squeaking go merrily on.

As we sat this bright morning in the market place, all at once, above the din, the church bells clanged. In an instant everything was dropped, the whole throng moved in solemn procession toward the church door, and Ahasuerus and I were left alone in the sunshine of the deserted plaza. We could hear the roll of the organ, the droning voice of the priest. A light breeze moved through the place, scattering the fragrance from the flower stalls; a little bird in the pepper-tree above our heads burst into song. "Truly," we said to each other, "Cholulu is a holy city."

The notes of the organ died away, the droning chant ceased, the church doors opened, and with an air of relief the bustling throng moved to their places, where the squawking of the cruelly handled fowl and the squealing of the bartered pigs began again—religion was done with, and business was on hand. And now came the Sunday bull-fight procession. This particular day it was a burlesque bull-fight, a sport which nevertheless meant torture and death to the poor dejected bull, who, covered with wreaths and garlands, headed the column. The toreadors who followed were clowns, with the familiar painted faces and the wide trousers of the American buffoon. They were succeeded by a bevy of hard-faced circus riders wearing their full skirts of the Mexican national colors, and by female charioteers, exchanging gibes with the crowd. As eagerly as they had flocked to the church at the sound of the bell, the crowd now flocked to see the fun, and the erstwhile devout church-goers disappeared under the arch of the bull-ring.

Ahasuerus and I, finding ourselves once more alone in the plaza, decided to enter one of the empty churches. But no sooner had we seated ourselves before the grand altar, beneath the cool shadow of the vaulted ceiling, than a crowd of beggars entered and surrounded us. They were evidently the impecunious ones who had not the price of admission to the bull-ring, and who saw in us the foreordained ministers to their pleasure. In vain we turned deaf ears to their solicitations. They became earnest, pressing, and finally even threatening in their demands, and we quitted our sacred retreat, saying to each other with a disgusted air, "Who is it that says Cholulu is a holy city?"

CHAPTER XIX.

The trip from Puebla to Oaxaca is a tiresome one, and only good travelers, with a philosophical disposition to make the best of things, should attempt it. We rose as usual by starlight, nibbled our crusts in the crowded station, and ensconced ourselves in the narrow-gauge cars. The first-class cars were shabby and dirty, but when we saw the second and third class ones we held our peace, and pondered on our mercies. And after all what did it matter, when outside the two white volcanoes were flushing in the dawn, when old Malintzi was catching the first glimmer of light on his snowy head, and, far, far away, across the plain, Orizaba was beginning to show his white peak like the tip of an angel's pinion?

For more than fifty miles we rode silent in the midst of this grandeur, and then all at once we entered a cañon where a little brook, bordered with green banks and waving boughs, cascaded beside us. In spite of our feasting eyes, however, we found the time from five o'clock in the morning until two o'clock in the afternoon a long fast, and were glad to break it with a sponge-cake which we bought of an enchanting dark-eyed maiden at one of the stations. The cake would have been really excellent if we could have forgotten the Indian woman who probably made it. We dined at last in a Chinese cabin with a dirt floor. The ceilings

A ZAPOTEC WOMAN.

were decorated with hams, bacon and graceful festoons of sausages, dried apples and onions. Outside the little brook chattered briskly, and the birds in the branches endeavored to drown its voice with their songs.

After leaving the dinner station we entered the cañon of San Antonio, and rode until dark between mountain walls lifting themselves thousands of feet above us. In our day's journey we descended into the torrid zone, with its coffee fields and waving palms and bananas, and rose again to the grain and corn fields of the temperate zone. We saw the natives washing gold from the bed of the cañon stream, and the husbandmen tilling with crooked sticks their little patches of ground, whose new-turned soil, pricked by the springing grain, curiously resembled porous-plasters upon the mountain side. We passed through quaint Indian villages whose picturesque inhabitants brought their wares to the station to sell, and watched the long burro trains patiently climbing the weary mountain passes. It was late in the evening when we at length reached Oaxaca and were met by a blessed American landlord, who took us to a blessed Ameriican hotel, where we ate once more the delightfully indigestible fried potato and drank our fill of the pure mountain water. No vintage in France or Italy knows the secret of that bouquet—the nectar of the gods—which after our long thirst we quaffed with the appetite of modern Jupiters. And here, too, in Oaxaca, we found the first really perfect climate we had seen in Mexico. All our heavy wraps came off and I reveled in the sunshine and in shirtwaists.

In spite of this eulogy, which sounds somewhat like the advertisement of a climatic resort, I own no springs and no real estate in Oaxaca, neither did I go there a wretched consumptive and return an athlete. I was not even the fortunate one to discover the peculiar advantages of the Oaxaca' soil and climate. That first-class judge of real estate, Cortés, was there before me, and among other trifles he obtained from the Spanish government a grant of the whole valley; and here, for a time, he made his home. But an older and a greater than Cortés and his band of adventurers has lived here —a nation whose civilization is forgotten, but whose ruined cities cover the hillsides around Oaxaca. This is the paradise of the archeologists, and the representatives of the New York Museum who had been prosecuting the researches in Yucatan were, at the time of our arrival in Oaxaca, endeavoring to unearth the secrets hidden in these mighty ruins. Some of the traditions concerning the buried cities are very interesting. On St. John's Day it is said that bells can be heard to ring from buried towers, and the Indians are very anxious to have the debris removed that they may find the bells.

Oaxaca was formerly the place to find genuine Aztec idols, but the Indians are beginning to understand their real value, and do not offer them so freely as formerly. Indeed, we were told by the intelligent woman who made the collection purchased by the New York Museum that many of the Indians love these sacred amulets and idols, and refuse to part with them at any price. "What?" exclaimed an old Indian to whom she made a proposition to purchase some of his treasures, "do you think I have no sense that I should sell my gods?" Poor benighted savage; he did not know that in a land, not far distant, there were people so anxious to get rid of their gods that they deliberately threw them away. But he will know better when he is civilized.

There is a fine Cathedral in Oaxaca which has fallen into the hands of a so-called decorator, and bids fair to be ruined. One of the most interesting of the churches is the ancient church of San Dominguey, which has a carved front and interior decorations of the most florid style. Florid decorations must, however, be expected in Mexico, and indeed they are suited to the people and the country. San Dominguey was confiscated by the government, and was for a time used as a barracks, and horses were stalled in its beautiful altars. It has, however, recently been returned to the Church, and at present is undergoing the painful process of restoration and redecoration. It is to be hoped that

PRESIDENT BENITO JUAREZ.

the fine bas-reliefs and other unique features of the interior will be spared.

One of the advertised charms of these tropical regions is the constellation of the Southern Cross.

The tradition of the Indian watchman, who at midnight calls "The Cross begins to bend," is a pretty one, but if the would-be astronomer wishes to see the Southern Cross in Oaxaca he must rise at some uncanny hour between two and four o'clock in the morning—an hour not at all adapted to star-gazing. Personally I am sufficiently loyal to my own latitude to consider the constellation of Orion far more beautiful than the vaunted Southern Cross.

Some of the greatest men in Mexico have been born in the State of Oaxaca. General Porfirio Diaz, the present president, was born in the little house on the outskirts of the town which is marked with a plaque. The great Juarez was a full-blooded Zapotec Indian. Until he was twelve years old he never heard a word of any language except his own Indian dialect. To learn the coveted Spanish tongue he bound himself out as a servant, and afterward in order to gain an education he entered the priesthood. But his path broadened before his feet, and he was called from the cell to take up the burdens of his people. He became governor of his state, then chief justice, and finally the president of the republic during her stormiest days. He repelled the French invasion, shot Maximilian, and gave to the world notice that Mexico would submit to no foreign dictation. He was the Mexican Washington who saved his country, and who, like

FERRY AT PUENTE REAL—page 225.

Washington, started it on a career of progress. He was the Mexican Bismarck, who, although himself a good Catholic, overthrew the political power of the Church, and established the public schools. He was the Mexican Lincoln—a conqueror, yet no soldier; a ruler, although scorned by the aristocrats; a hero, yet a simple man of the people, who understood him and supported him and loved him. I never see his plain, dark face without a thrill of the same reverent affection I feel for Lincoln, and I am persuaded that among the great names of the earth the name of Benito Juarez should stand very near the head.

CHAPTER XX.

Again and again we made ready for our trip to Mitla; again and again we rose at an untimely hour in the morning and sat patiently waiting for a carriage that never came. In vain Ahasuerus pleaded and offered bribes; in vain the friendly landlord argued, threatened and uttered maledictions; not the least ripple was stirred on the current of Mexican movement. But at last, as I sat one morning forlornly watching, a rattle as of the dead bones of a nation was heard afar down the street, and soon after, with a clatter and a jangle, four desiccated mules were reined up at the door. In an instant two sombrero-hatted figures descended, each seized a stone, and crawling under the carriage began vigorously to hammer at the crazy bolts. We, with a firm determination to trust the bolts to Providence, climbed joyfully to our seats and finally persuaded the reluctant coachman to drive on. At last *manana* was come and we were on our way to Mitla.

The drive of twenty-five miles from Oaxaca to

Mitla is not a comfortable one. In these regions we are only seventeen degrees north of the equator, further south than either Cairo or Calcutta. A tropical sun beats down upon the head, the air swims with dust, and the jolt of the cobblestone pavements which extend to the outermost limits of Oaxaca is bone-racking.

As we advanced into the open country we found

ON THE ROAD TO MITLA.

the road lined with Zapotec Indians bringing their produce to market. The Zapotecs, although the degenerate descendants of a nobler ancestry, are nevertheless a much finer race than the Aztecs of the valley of Mexico. The original Zapotecs were an arrogant people who claimed descent from the rocks and the lions. At the time of the coming of Cortés they were waging successful warfare with the powerful Aztecs, but they as well as their Indian foemen were compelled to bend to the yoke of the Spaniard. The graceful, veiled figure of the modern Zapotec woman perched between the high-piled panniers on the donkey's back resembles the pictures we see of the Jewish women of the Old Testament. When she walks she goes, even when carrying the heaviest burdens, upon a fox trot. To see one of these lithe figures advancing, her head held splendidly erect under the jar or basket, her garments fluttering in the wind, her willowy body undulating, and her bare feet scarce touching the ground is to see Greek art embodied.

A few miles from Oaxaca we passed through Tule, which is, with its rows of mud huts, its nearly naked children, and its hordes of half-starved dogs, a typical Indian village. The little town is famous for its big tree, a species of cypress, which in diameter exceeds the far-famed California big trees. The half-obliterated inscription upon the trunk is said to have been cut by the great Humboldt. As we drove through the village we saw the municipal school gathered in the cloisters of the church, studying aloud with a buzz like a hive of bees. The little garden plots and fields of this region are hedged with the organa or organ-pipe cactus which sometimes grows twenty feet high, and is said to yield delicious fruit.

By the advice of our big-hatted coachman, who seemed to exist for the purpose of shutting off the air and the view, and to speak for the purpose of misleading us, we stopped for luncheon at the vil-

AN ORGANA HEDGE.

lage of Tlacolulu. Everything was very convenient at Tlacolulu. The washstand, flanked by a row of soiled towels tastefully arranged, stood at the head of the table in the dining-room, so that we could wash, eat, drink and be merry with the least possible loss of time. There is a church in Tlacolulu which, according to the guide-book, is famous for its antiquity. I really believe that it antedates the towels, but it is no less ugly for that; and the women sitting on a heap of sand, called by courtesy the market place, were pictures of sordid and unromantic misery. On the whole Tlacolulu seems to possess all the objectionable features of a poor Mexican Indian town with none of the picturesqueness which makes such a village tolerable.

Upon our arrival in Mitla we were hospitably received by the dark-faced Mexican Don who is the fortunate proprietor of the hacienda and the Indian village in which are found the ruins of Mitla. The front of the hacienda house is used as a shop for the supply of the simple needs of the village. We passed through an arched entrance to the beautiful court beyond, upon whose broad corridors all the rooms of the house opened. An enormous bougainvillea vine draped one side of the court with a mantle of purple. On the opposite side of the patio a group of Indian women and children were industriously engaged in hulling and sorting green coffee beans. Apart from its beauty I shall always remember this hacienda as one of the few hostelries in the rural districts of Mexico where we were given clean table linen. At Don Felix Quéro's we had not only snowy linen, but well-cooked, well-served meals, sweetened by the most hospitable welcome of the master and the mistress of the house.

The sun's rays were level when we waded through the deep sand, past the thatched huts and the dirty stable yards, decorated with queer wooden-wheeled carts, to the ruins. An ignorant custodian led the way, endeavoring to impart in a villainous dialect as much misinformation as he thought we could be induced to bear, while a crowd of persistent and pestilent Indian beggars dogged our footsteps. As we were conscious, however, that the foolish alms-giving of our own Americans was responsible for the latter annoyance, we endured the attacks of the pertinacious rabble with what grace we could.

The ruins are more extensive than at first sight they seem. Many of the village huts are built upon the fallen walls with fragments stolen from the temples. In spite, however, of the work of the vandals, enough of Mitla remains to give a distinct idea of the original beauty of the edifices. Indeed, some of the structures are almost intact, presenting a style of architecture at once simple and majestic. Nothing in Rome thrilled me as did those solid windowless walls, glistening in the level rays of the sun.

The walls, which are about six feet thick, are of

small pebbles bound together with lasting cement. Upon this is laid a veneer of carved stone, and immense blocks of the same stone form the sills and the lintels of the doorway. Both the interior and the exterior of the buildings are ornamented

A CRUMBLING WALL.

with broad bands of the stone overlaid with stone mosaics cut in geometrical and fantastic patterns. The Toltecs, the supposed builders of Mitla, had no arch in their architecture; consequently the doorways are all square, a style which gives one the impression of massiveness, as, indeed, does every detail of the huge piles. The Hall of the Monoliths, which Humboldt pronounced one of the wonders of the new world, contains six gigantic stone columns without base or capital.

One of the temples is occupied by an Indian family, who cook their food on a smoky brazier in one corner of the room, and stable their donkey and cow in another corner. The walls of this unique dwelling are covered with whitewash, which, at the command of the custodian, was in one spot rubbed off, revealing a glistening band of dark-red cement. This band, which encircles the room, is covered with hieroglyphics, which are crumbling and rapidly disappearing. Before the archeologists succeed in finding the key and deciphering the records, the records will be gone, and with them will go the secrets of the great temple builders.

A flight of crumbling steps leads to the hill which was once crowned by the teocalli and the sacrificial stone of the Toltecs, where they offered to the gods human hearts torn from the bodies of their writhing victims. The proselyting Spaniards destroyed the temple with its valuable records, and with the material from the ruin built upon the same spot a shabby church. The mutilation begun by the Spaniard is continued by the Mexican and the Indian. A year ago a tomb containing human remains was found and thriftily turned by the villagers into a corn bin. The former custodian—an old priest who fully appreciated the beauty and value of the ruins—endeavored to protect them from injury. In retaliation the Indians—who consider themselves entitled to all the benefits accruing from the possession of so great a treasure, cut off his water supply, stole his fruit and chickens, and in other ways made his life so miserable that he was only too glad to resign and leave Mitla to its fate.

It is much to be wished that the proprietor of Mitla would employ as custodian one who has some intelligent knowledge of the remains, and who could speak some other language than the half-Indian, half-Spanish dialect of the present caretaker. When the old man discovered that we could not comprehend his jargon, he inquired rather superciliously if we spoke French; but upon hearing our delighted affirmative, his enthusiasm waned, and I found that his French vocabulary consisted of "Oui, Madame," and "Non, Madame."

It is now conceded by archeologists that Mitla was the seat of the hierarchy and the burial place of the kings. The people who built these massive piles, cut the huge stones, and carved the mosaics must have been of a high type of civilization. When Cortés came to Mexico he found in the country no beasts of burden. The quarries, from which the stones used in the construction of the temples of Mitla doubtless came, are five miles away. How did men, by their own unassisted efforts, raise these huge stones and transport them a distance of five miles? Surely not enough men to lift one of the blocks could find place around it. The ancient

SPECIMENS OF MOSAIC.

builders, then, must have possessed some machinery for lifting heavy weights, the knowledge of whose construction might be valuable even to us. We of these golden days, when confronted by the mysteries of past civilizations, may well doubt if we are really the heirs of all the ages. There may be hidden codicils which, if ever discovered, will prove to us that we have not yet inherited all the wisdom of the centuries.

We ate our supper in the little dining-room looking out into the darkening court. The maidens of the household came, with their gracefully poised water jars, to the fountain, and a troop of horses plunged through the arched entrance and curveted across the court to get their evening drink. One by one the swinging lamps blazed out along the garlanded porch; the children's evening hymn floated up from the little shrine at the end of the corridor, and from the servants' quarters across the court arose the sweet strains of the Ave Maria. We sat among the blossoms until the moon rode high in the heavens and the stars stooped almost to the touch of our fingers. Then we went into the thick-walled, barred-windowed cells which served as sleeping rooms, and throwing ourselves upon the hard pallets, slept until morning. I was awakened by a gentle neigh, and opening my eyes I saw an inquiring pony and a velvet-nosed donkey gazing timidly and curiously through the grating upon my slumbers. I arose, caressed my gentle visitors, and went blithely out into an ungrateful world, which has blotted out the memory and trodden down the handiwork of the ancient builders.

CHAPTER XXI.

The impressions of a traveler are not always reliable, but for those journeying as we journeyed, often the only English-speaking people on the train, staying at Mexican hotels, riding on Mexican street cars, and in all ways affiliating with the native population, there are opportunities for hearing both sides of vexed questions that escape the hasty tourist or one who journeys in his private car. Then, too, as I was generally the only woman in sight, I personally received a great deal of courteous and kindly information from members of the superior sex, who, whatever their nationality, were always willing to enlighten my ignorance according to the most improved kindergarten methods. We also talked much with railroad men—conductors, ticket agents and engineers—who, in the dearth of responsible native workmen and officials, are sent from the United States to Mexico. These men are generally wan-eyed and baldheaded, having lost their hair in the fever, and most of them are homesick and dissatisfied. Above all things they fear the fever, and they warned us against everything; against the water, against the night air, and particularly against the fruit. Fever, however, is not the worst thing to be feared in Mexico, for we encountered both malignant diphtheria and smallpox. Indeed, judging from the scarred and seamed faces seen on all sides, smallpox is the universal heritage, and vaccination unknown in the republic.

Begging is another form of virulent disease that afflicts Mexico, but we were told that Americans are largely responsible for this malady. When an excursion party is expected, the thrifty Mexican mothers clothe their children in rags and send them to the train. The tender-hearted Americans, moved by the pitiful sight, shower pennies upon the poor innocents, and the Mexican families live for weeks in comfort upon the money thus gained. This spread of pauperism by indiscriminate alms-giving is a theme for meditation, for if it be really true that we Americans are offenders in this respect, we may be sure that, sooner or later, we shall be compelled to pay the penalty of our thoughtlessness.

During our return trip from Oaxaca I had a chance to study the methods of a "general promoter of industries" and other schemes, who spoke as one having authority, and who was particularly eulogistic of the Mexicans. As he had the appearance of not having bathed for several years I thought that some parts of La Republica were specially adapted to his needs. He did not, however, agree with us in our high estimate of the southern Indian. "I tell you," he said, "one of them northern Indians at Chihuahua is wuth a dozen of them southern fellows. Jest give 'em plenty of pulque, and cornmeal, and a cigar or so, and they'll work like a mule; they'll work till they drop." From the point of view of the "general promoter," the northern Indian is certainly the better man.

The consensus of opinion seems to be that the Mexicans, whether of the north or of the south, have little mechanical ingenuity, and that they cannot be trusted to care for machinery. The Spanish lack of caution which ruined the engines of Cervera's fleet is also characteristic of the half-breed Mexican. A strike on one of the railways last winter, which compelled the road to employ Mexican engineers, resulted in the burning out of most of the engines, and the general demoralization of the rolling stock. This lack of trustworthiness is apparent in all grades of railway service. One of the first things we noticed upon our arrival in Mexico was the fact that the switchman always stood with one foot on the switch until the train had passed. We learned afterward that, as the Mexican cannot be trusted to set a switch and lock it, he is compelled by law to stand with his foot upon the bar; for only the certainty that in case of an accident he will be the first one killed, has the power to make a native switchman responsible.

Nor is this lack of reliability confined to the lower classes, for, I am sorry to say, the American, English and German mine-owners and capitalists whom, we met, made the same complaint of Mexican business men. So far as their integrity is concerned we personally, with the exception of our experience with the Vera Cruzans, who, like the people of most seaport towns, are a shifting and a shifty population—found no one disposed to deal dishonestly with us; indeed we suffered less imposition than we should be liable to meet on a similar trip in our own country. It is evident, however, that the average Mexican cannot keep an appointment—a weakness imputed to the Spanish race everywhere. Some American capitalists whom we met in Aguas Calientes told us that they had been waiting in town since Monday (it was then Thursday) for a Mexican mine-owner with whom they had a business appointment.

The return journey from Puebla to the City of Mexico carries us past Cholulu, thence onward near the foot of the volcanoes, and by a tramway from the station of Santa Ana, to the ancient republic of Tlaxcala, whose inhabitants Cortés secured as allies in his conflict with the Aztecs. Of these Tlaxcalans, then numbering over 300,000 souls, whose valor in battle so impressed Cortés that he hastened to make friends with them, only about 4,000 remain. The old town, which was built in an amphitheater, in the foothills, is one of the notable places in Mexico. In the ancient church of San Francisco, built in 1521, is still preserved the oldest pulpit in America, and in the Casa Municipale is the original grant of arms given to the Tlaxcalans by Charles V., the standard given to the Tlaxcalan chiefs by Cortés, and the robes in which the chiefs were baptized.

At San Martin we begin to climb the mountains, and at Naucamilca we reach the highest point, 9,000 feet above the sea. These high regions are one vast field of waving grain, and white-walled haciendas dot the landscape. At the lower elevation of 6,000 feet we find ourselves once more among the green spikes of the maguey, and see and smell on all sides the yeasty liquor. Nearing the Capital we pass the Pyramids of the Sun and the Moon, and whirl along the low banks of Lake Texcoco. At Chapingo is one of the finest haciendas in Mexico, the property of the heirs of President Gonzales, the one-armed patriot and boodler who preceded Diaz. Beyond Chapingo we enter a long avenue of mighty trees, through whose drooping branches the city lights begin to glimmer. The glimmer livens to a glow, and at last in a dazzle of electric lamps we enter the St. Lazare station. Once more we feel ourselves a part of the civilization of the nineteenth century, and as we sink back on the comfortable cushions of the carriage we are

THE BURDEN BEARERS.

glad to forget for a time Cortés, the Aztecs, Quetzalcoatl, and all the other dead and gone gods and heroes. We eat our well-cooked dinner in a modern French restaurant, and we wipe our mouths, and we say "ah-ha," for we feel in every fiber of our beings that we are the children of steam and electricity, daily newspapers, and modern cooking and service.

CHAPTER XXII.

We left the Capital one bright morning in March by the daybreak train on the Mexican National R. R. and journeyed eastward one hundred and twenty-five miles, as far as the station of San Marcos. Here we left the train and sat for five wretched hours in a miserable little station house, while the deaf, the halt, the blind, the horribly disfigured, strolling peddlers and curiosity seekers came to gaze upon the *Americanos*. At the sight of the misery around me it really seemed that I owed heaven and humanity some apology for physical and mental vigor, and for all my worldly comforts. Nevertheless these pious reflections did not prevent a feeling of sickness when in the midst of these unappetizing surroundings I tried to swallow my lunch. Ahasuerus went out and bought a bottle of Spanish wine to complete the meal. The memory of that acid drink still sets my teeth on edge and chills the blood in my veins, but the starving creatures to whom we gave it, with the remains of the lunch, swallowed it with a heart-breaking avidity. It is difficult for an American accustomed to the abundance of his own land to realize that in our neighboring republic many people annually die of starvation.

The train on the branch road which leads to the foot of the mountains started about the middle of the day. We found the first-class cars had cushioned seats along each side and in dimensions and comfort much resembled a small American omnibus. We were fortunate enough to have two very interesting traveling companions, one a sprightly young Mexican in the early twenties, the other a magnificently handsome Spaniard of about forty-five. The Mexican wore the skin-tight jacket and trousers of the gay young native who fondly imagines he is wearing "American clothes." The Spaniard was attired in a suit of Mexican cut, made of silver-gray broadcloth and ornamented with an infinity of silver buttons, chains and loops. Upon his head was a high sombrero of gray fur-felt, bearing upon the front a monogram in silver, and upon his feet were gaiters of gray ooze leather. The costume was admirably calculated to set off his dark beauty, and I have never seen, outside of a frame, a more glorious picture than this Spaniard. Like many very handsome men, he seemed entirely unconscious of his charms, but gave his mind to the admiring and reflective contemplation of some specimens of ore which he drew from a silver-decked pouch at his side.

We soon discovered that both men were mine owners, who naturally believed that they had a fortune in their mines. They were disposed to be very friendly, and we were soon included in their stately and courteous conversation. As our knowledge of the Spanish tongue did not extend beyond the words and phrases necessary for our daily travel and needs, we were somewhat bewildered at the jargon of "ores," "assays," and other mining terms. We endeavored, however, to look as intelligent as possible, smiled, beamed with our best American beam, and murmured intermittently "Si, Señor," and I'm sure I hope we said it in the right place.

We reached our destination—a little Indian village—after dark. Tired and hungry, we welcomed the feebly burning lights of the tiny hamlet, and, forgetting for the moment that we were in Mexico, Ahasuerus demanded of the conductor the way to the nearest hotel. It was an unfortunate slip of the tongue, and when the conductor, who for a wonder understood him, pointed to a miserable fonda not far from the station, the naked truth was too bitter for us. I fancied that I saw a bit of mockery in the smile with which the Spaniard said, "The Señora

likes not the hotel?—so?"—a fancy which nerved me to walk up to the wretched place with an air of placidity, although at each step my heart sank lower and lower. The inn, which was of two stories, was a crazy building leaning to the wind in a perilous manner. The lower floor was of dirt and the upper one of loose boards. Along the upper balcony were strung lines of bloody sheep-skins, sickening alike to the eyes and to the nostrils. An Indian woman, the mistress of the house, and too evidently the mistress of its Spanish master, conducted us up the shaking stairway to a room containing two beds; one for Ahasuerus and myself, the other for our traveling companion, the young Mexican. "Well," said that worm Ahasuerus, turning upon me as soon as we were left alone, "you are fond of romantic adventures and picturesque scrapes. How do you like this?"

He soon strolled off, grumbling, and left me with my handkerchief to my nose and despair in my heart, ensconced in one corner of the porch behind the gory sheepskins. From my nook I overheard a discussion between the Indian landlady and our fellow-travelers. "But," argued the young Mexican, "the señora does not like it; it is not the custom of her country." The woman, who spoke an Indian dialect unintelligible to me, was evidently impervious to the señora's likes and dislikes, for neither man seemed to affect her decision. I soon withdrew, and I knew the result of the discussion only from what followed. When we went to bed we left the candle burning and the door open for our roommate, but when we woke in the morning we found that he had not been in. On my way to breakfast, as I passed a large room, I recognized among the rugs and blankets strewn over the floor the Mexican's portmanteau, and I realized the fact that rather than annoy us he had slept with the rougher guests of the fonda upon the dirty floor.

When the pangs of hunger overcame us we went, one at a time, lest we should carry down the crazy stairway, to look for dinner. We entered a large room with a dirt floor, which was filled with the smoke of braziers. At one end of the room was a long table, covered with a coffee-stained cloth, at which sat seven or eight evil-faced, bandit-looking men, who, in spite of their unprepossessing appearance, rose courteously upon our entrance to salute us. Across the other end of the room was a stone table in which were inserted the barred braziers upon which the dinner was cooking. The coals and cinders continually dropped between the bars of the braziers upon the dirt floor, to the peril of a troop of ragged, unkempt children, the offspring of the Indian woman and her Spanish master, who stood lowering in the doorway, as ugly a specimen of brutal humanity as I ever looked upon. A stone bench upon which the woman—a tiny creature—climbed to reach the steaming kettles, was in front of the range. The heavy vessels were unbearable weights in the woman's feeble hands, and she stumbled awkwardly up and down the bench, to the disgust of her lord, who continually cursed her. Around the table were stone benches upon which we, with the other guests, seated ourselves. Some hungry kittens, two half-starved dogs and a brood of piping chickens disputed with us the possession of this seat.

I have eaten worse meals, even in the United States, than this dinner in the Mexican fonda. There was no drinking water, but, as usual in such inns, a large bottle of pulque was placed before each cover. The soup course was really delicious, the omelet good and the frijoles appetizing, so that we were enabled to make a bountiful meal. It is true that the time between courses was rather long, but the guests showed the most exemplary patience, and evinced their friendly interest by offering advice or suggestions to the tiny cook, and they seemed to like the food no less that they had a hand in its preparation.

Our traveling companions, who had in the meantime joined us, in deference to our American prejudices removed their hats; but the other men sat, silent and haughty, under the shadow of their great sombreros. The light from a smoky lantern upon the wall fell upon the heads and the gloomy shadowed faces of the diners, and I was reminded of a gypsy scene in an opera. The only thing lacking to the theatrical effect of the whole was the orchestral accompaniment. In spite of the picturesqueness of the scene, however, I must confess that I could not repress a thrill of fear at noticing that Ahasuerus was the only unarmed man in the company. The other guests carried heavy pistols swinging from their cartridge belts, and the ring of their revolvers upon the stone benches formed a martial accompaniment to the jingle of spurs that gave me an uncomfortable impression of being among the bandits; an impression which the fierce faces of the Mexican caballeros in no way belied. I lay down that night, for the only time in Mexico, with a feeling of uneasiness; but the sole disturbers of our peace were the chickens, pigs, donkeys and horses beneath us, whose high-keyed chorus ascended through the wide cracks of the rough floor.

Our awakening was cheered by the appearance of our friend and expectant host, who reported the coming of a horse for Ahasuerus, and a band of Indian chairmen to carry me over the mountains. They had, he assured us, started early in the night and would soon arrive; so we hastily dispatched our rolls and coffee, and sat us patiently down to await the burden-bearers. One by one the swarthy guests of the fonda departed; our traveling com-

ACROSS THE MOUNTAINS.

panions, with many "addios" and graceful salutations, jingled off to their mines, and still the Indians did not come. It was nearly noon when they finally appeared with the chariot which was to transport me to higher regions. This chariot was a high-backed wooden chair with a broad foot rest, and a white cotton canopy overhead which could be drawn over the face or thrown back.

I seated myself in the chair, the Indian porter knelt, placed one of the two bands around his forehead, and the other around his shoulders, rose slowly like a camel and trotted off with me. The motion was delightful—much like the easy canter of a pony—and many a sly nap I took under my white canopy as the day wore on. There were four chairmen who relieved one another at stated intervals. They were all strong, robust Indians accustomed to burdens of at least two hundred and fifty pounds, so that my conscience did not too much reprove me, although I must confess that I had all the time the feeling that I was making of a human soul a beast of burden. The beasts of burden, however, bore their load cheerfully; for the first one carried me, in spite of my protests, straight up the mountain five miles without stopping. Besides our Indian retainers we were accompanied by our host's mozo, or private servant, and three gaunt Indian dogs who serenely trod the path of glory, giving triumphant battle to all the other dogs in the various Indian villages through which we passed.

We traveled during the day over three mountain ranges. Up and down the steep declivities, skirting the narrow benches, threading the rocky ravines, and descending green valleys in whose verdant depths were hidden Indian villages, went the sure-footed mountain horses, and my bearers traveled close upon their heels. We often exchanged greetings with the dignified Aztecs, ploughing in the green fields and upon the rocky slopes, fishing in the tumbling streams, or gathered around the adobe schoolhouses and the tiny cross-crowned churches, and we always received from these humble, native señors a courteous, if a curious, salutation.

The sun was setting as we wound slowly down the mountain trail into the little Indian village nestling at the foot of the third range. The men working in the fields and the women washing at the fountain turned to look at us, while a graceful girl, who was driving a flock of black goats, in her astonishment allowed a little jet-faced kid to escape and to run, crying like a baby, after us. One of the Indian guides seized the little creature and turned its head in the opposite direction, whereupon it fled, wailing, back to its mother. The whole scene was one of pastoral innocence, and with sighs of happy content we pressed onward, down the verdant valley to the spot where the home of our host—the only white man in the village—nestled among the trees beside the tiny mission church and schoolhouse.

We had scarcely removed from our clothing the dust of travel, when we were told that visitors were waiting to see us. We descended and were greeted by the head man of the village—a courteous and intelligent Indian—and the master of the municipal school. They had come to bid us wel-

DESCENT INTO THE VALLEY.

come to their town, and to offer their services for our entertainment. Although the Aztec was their native tongue they spoke Spanish musically and fluently. The schoolmaster had not at all the physique of the Indian. His face was round, his eyes were sparkling, and he had altogether the air of a fat, jolly negro. Both men wore the American dress; that is to say they both wore coats and trousers, although hardly of the American cut. Their heads were covered with the straw sombrero so universally worn by the Indians.

The village, which numbers about 1,500 souls, is hidden away in this lost corner of the earth, where the ancestors of the people took refuge from the fury of Cortés. Three centuries later, upon the coming of Maximilian, the tribe burned their villages and hid in the mountain fastnesses, so that they have a perfect right to proclaim themselves an unconquered people whose adherence to the Mexican republic is entirely voluntary. They certainly have all the physical traits of an unconquered race and are the tallest and finest Indians we saw in Mexico. Unlike other tribes, they all own their little farms, which they cultivate, by means of crooked sticks and placid, thick-necked oxen, to the very summit of the mountains. Although courteous and affable to strangers, they are at enmity with all the Indian villages further down the mountain, whose inhabitants profess the Catholic faith—the hated faith of the Spaniard. A handful of the tribe has been gathered into the Protestant mission, but the majority are without religion.

They keep many of their old customs in this faraway corner of the world. The women still spin with distaffs and weave with curious handlooms. Doubtless their untroubled lives, as well as the mountain air, contribute to their longevity; certainly we saw many very old people. The dress of the men consists of the usual straw sombrero,

AZTEC LOOM—FOUR GENERATIONS.

wide linen trousers, and a linen shirt, reaching halfway to the knees girded around the waist by a bright scarf. The women wear skirts and chemises whose low cut reveals beautiful shoulders generally ornamented with curious bead necklaces, and they have no head covering except the rebosa and their dark tresses. Neither sex wears shoes, and both men and women possess slender, high-arched feet which are, in spite of the usual coating of dust, of wonderful beauty. A curious custom prevails among the men and boys of wearing one trouser leg rolled almost to the thigh, revealing a slender, shining limb. When questioned as to the reason for this, they could only answer: "It is the fashion"—an answer that proves the mountain Indian to be on the highway to civilization. The houses of the village, which are of mud or adobe, stuccoed, and painted some bright tint, stand in the midst of neat gardens, the streets are well kept, the children clean and pretty, and the people themselves are industrious and contented.

CHAPTER XXIII.

The morning after our arrival in the village we went with our host to the Sunday services held in the little adobe church, which during the week serves him also for a schoolhouse. Our friend—a graceful and fluent speaker—preached to the little flock in Spanish; although, as many of the people know only the Aztec, the services of an interpreter are often called into requisition. The congregation seemed teachable and intelligent, and we noticed many handsome faces among the women. We were exceedingly interested in the school which we visited next day. There were ninety scholars—a fine beginning for a school so recently established. The school and the mission, which are supported by the Methodist Church, are under the supervision of our friend and host.

The dream of this good man is the establishment of an industrial school and farm for the training of these mountain Indians. The Jéfé Politico, or

MORELOS—*page 248.*

head man of the district—a man of wealth and cultivation—sympathizes with him in his ambition, and will doubtless give him practical aid. The high-class Mexicans are mostly Protestants, or rather protesters against the Romish Church, and this prejudice against Catholicism extends to the Indians of the entire district; so that in a population of 29,000 souls there are but three priests, and these are by no means welcome. How far this sentiment against the faith of the Spaniards will carry the mountaineers remains to be seen; but certainly at present there seems to be a decided inclination to affiliate with the Protestant church, and to lend to our friend a helping hand in his work. This sentiment was most kindly shown on the occasion of the baptism of the missionary's baby boy. The Jéfé Politico of the district, who with his wife acted as godparents to the little American, came, accompanied by two Indian orchestras, thirty miles over a rough and dangerous mountain road, to the ceremony. The wife, who was not able to come, in accordance with Mexican customs sent her sister to represent her, and to bring the christening offering of a cloak and hood for the little one. One hundred and fifty guests were present, and the festivities lasted three days. The pretty baby received from his friend, the Jéfé Politico, a copy of a Spanish Testament around which were knotted the Mexican and American flags fastened together with clasped silver hands.

We went one day upon the invitation of the schoolmaster to visit the municipal school. This is one of the schools which the paternal policy of the Mexican government has established in every town and village of the republic. When we presented ourselves at the schoolhouse, the scholars were enjoying their recess upon the shaded playgrounds. We were received with the most graceful and gracious hospitality by the schoolmaster, who wore ragged trousers and a soiled shirt, through whose torn sleeves his mighty arms shone like polished bronze. His massive head, with its close-cropped, clustering locks, was poised upon his columnar neck, with that combination of strength and freedom that we see in the statues of the Greek gods. This simple Indian, who knew nothing of the world beyond his mountains, except what he had learned from books, was an impressive and a majestic figure.

The walls of the schoolroom were hung with French plates, geometrical, mechanical, physiological and scientific. Pictures of the birds, beasts, flowers, shells and insects of all lands were there, as well as those of the organs of the human body, designs of modern machinery, lithographs of domestic and prehistoric animals, mountain ranges, river courses, and portraits of famous men. The collection was a picture book on a magnificent scale for the fortunate children.

We were taken first to a little room set apart for manual work. Here the clay molding, the wood carving, and the paper cutting filled us with astonishment. We went next to the garden where the children playing under the trees greeted us courteously, and withdrew to a distance that they might not seem to listen to our conversation. This school also numbered about ninety scholars, all intelligent and vivacious. Playing quietly and modestly among the others was the great grandson of a famous Mexican general who had served with distinguished honor in the armies of the republic. This little scion of a noble house was a pretty five-year-old boy, with a bright manly face. Around the garden were rows of blooming flower-beds cared for by the children, who were each given a garden plot to cultivate, and thus learned to associate with the school curriculum that expert knowledge of agriculture which will in the future be so important an interest to them.

When we returned to the schoolhouse the master blew upon a whistle, and seating himself at a melancholy, wheezing melodeon, played a spirited march. The children entered in a procession, clapping their hands together to mark the time, and after various evolutions and some creditable singing, took their places at their desks, after which the regular routine of the schoolroom went on, while we sat by and marveled. A class in drawing copied the figures on the walls, and drew the chair and inkstand, which the master placed for the purpose in different posi-

THE MISSION CHURCH.

tions. The work was naturally of various degrees of excellence, but none of it was absolutely poor.

A class of beginners in geography was called up. Each of the children—aged from eight to ten years —was asked to give the number of his house (every house on every crossroad in Mexico is numbered), then the name of the street on which he lived, and the name of the municipality. "Who are the officers of the municipality?" was the next question, and then "What are the duties of those officers?" The duties of the municipal officers as defined by the children are first, to provide water; then make roads; furnish street lamps, afterward build bridges, and keep the streets clean. No mention whatever was made of sewers, for the Mexicans have not yet learned the necessity for them. From the municipality the children were led on to the district in which they lived, its officers and their duties, and finally to the officers of the republic. "In time," said the teacher, "they will make excursions into other countries, thus learning geography, history and national law from the starting point of their own front doors. My methods of teaching in all branches," continued the schoolmaster, entirely unconscious of our ill-concealed amazement, "are Socratic. I never tell a child a truth; I let him find it out for himself. When his premises are wrong I question him until he sees where his argument leads him." Please bear in mind that this man was an Indian—one of the race we are accustomed to call savages.

It is also well to remember that the children, until the age of six years, had heard and spoken the

Aztec tongue only, and that knowledge came to them through the medium of the acquired Spanish language. Yet the geography class showed an intelligent interest in the duties and responsibilities of official life that augurs well for the wisdom of the future aldermen and governors of Mexico.

The writing class, composed of twelve-year-old boys and girls, wrote at the dictation of our host, a rapid script, as clear as engraving. One of the boys, at the dictation of the master, wrote the following sentence in Spanish upon his slate, and presented the slate to me. "We are glad to have the Americans come among us and bring the refining influences of civilization." I blushed, as I read the kindly sentiment, remembering some of the influences of civilization brought by my people to his race further north.

The schoolmaster listened to our encomiums with an air of modest doubt. "If I could only go to your country," he said wistfully, in his rich Spanish—"but I never shall; so I must work it out myself." As we went down the street, we looked back, and saw him standing thoughtfully in the doorway—a grand figure in his shabby garments—and I thought of the many Americans I had known to whom years of college and foreign university life had not given that discipline of the intellect, that real education which had been acquired by this poor

Indian "working it out" in his lonely home on the distant mountain.

The time came all too soon when we were obliged to leave this peaceful valley. At the time of our departure we had another experience of the procrastinating policy of the Mexicans. The head

THE "DECENT FONDA."

man of the village, who was deputed to engage the chairmen for our trip down the mountains, had done nothing in the matter, and as we were not disposed to wait for his slow bargaining, I made the descent on horseback. If the ascent had been hard on the Indian bearers, the descent was hard on me, for the combination of comfortless Mexican saddle and constant downward pitch reduced me, mentally as well as physically, to a jelly-like consistency. The night overtook us long before we reached the plains, and we rode in the dark, seemingly for endless hours, along the edge of a bottomless abyss, while the mountain whip-poor-will made mournful music to our misery. When we, at last, arrived before the door of the decent little fonda, which our host had recommended to us, I slipped, a boneless mass, from the saddle and bewailed my fate. But everybody was very good to me; the horses and the donkeys rubbed their velvet noses sympathizingly against my face, the Indian dogs rallied to my support, and the Indian woman of the fonda stayed me with flagons and comforted me with apples—in other words, she brought to my room a cup of varnish-like coffee and a crust of hard bread, and I slept as sweetly upon my wooden pallet as if it had been a bed of down.

We had upon our journey to San Marcos the next morning some fellow-passengers who were very different from our former traveling companions. The youngest member of this party of four had a face like that of one of Raphael's young saints. From their conversation we learned that the men were cock-fighters returning from a *professional* trip in the mountains. They drank whisky incessantly—not at all a common custom among the Mexicans—and their conversation and manner showed the greatest depravity. I grieve to say that the saintly faced young fellow was the most reckless of the company. One cannot always judge the flavor of an apple from the color of its skin.

CHAPTER XXIV.

We looked our last upon the Capital one hot afternoon and climbed the mountains in the trail of the old brigands, to where Toluca sits in the shadow of her dead volcano. Along the road were caves hollowed in the mountain sides to which the Indians, during the rainy season, retreat from the inundations in the valley below. Above our heads towered Monte Cruces, or the Mount of Crosses, so called from the numerous headstones on the summit which mark the graves of the bandits and their victims. At our feet danced the Lerma River, and far off down the valley glowed the windows of the little villages reflecting the light of the setting sun. The views on this route are wondrously beautiful, and it was with regret that we saw the sun dip below the horizon. But Toluca had no need of the sun to lighten it, for electricity did the work perfectly. I doubt if there is a better lighted city in the United States. The government buildings are the finest in the republic, the zocalo and the market place are worthy of attention, the *portales* are wide and spotless, the streets are clean, and, best of all, the air that sweeps through them is fresh and sweet. In fact Toluca needs only a comfortable hotel to make it in the eyes of travelers one of the very best of Mexican cities.

The City of Mexico is the capital of the Republic,

A MOUNTAIN HOME.

but Toluca is the capital of the State of Mexico. The latter city, although really very ancient, is, in many ways, more modern than the former, which takes on nineteenth century methods slowly and sullenly. Toluca, on the contrary, has an air of wide-awake progressiveness which I hope is not deceptive; at all events as a proof of her early enterprise she shows, in one of her chapels, a shabby little organ said to have been the first organ ever built in America. It is true that her people still cling to a miraculous and horrible image of the Virgin painted on unnecessarily coarse cloth, to the bull-ring and to many of their old traditions, but electric lights, ready-made clothing, free schools and a brewery, if not all civilizing, are wonderfully Americanizing institutions, and Toluca has all these. Above the city rises more than 15,000 feet the extinct volcano Nevado, which can be ascended by the traveler. The trip takes about two days. The crater is a bottomless pit of water with a whirlpool and other attendant horrors.

We were roused from our slumbers one chilly midnight to follow the *camerista* through the brightly lighted *portales* of the sleeping town to the street car. Here we sat in somnolent state for more than half an hour, while belated citizens and policemen bearing dimly burning lanterns through the illuminated streets, came to gaze upon us. In the eyes of these night prowlers, all heavily armed, we, with our harmless equipment of handbags and umbrella straps, must have seemed like a delegation from the peace party. Fortunately the delegation feared nothing from the warlike demonstrations around them, for human life is sacred in Mexico, where the government considers itself responsible for the protection of strangers. We knew that not long before the Mexican republic had paid in damages a heavy sum to the family of an American who had been murdered by a native, and we were sure that not one of the dashing young swash-bucklers of Toluca would dare use his silver-decked revolver except in an extremity. The life of the poorest peon is as carefully guarded as that of an official, a fact which proves that at the core Mexico, in spite of its one-man dynasty, is more truly republican than we are.

After a weary wait in the darkness, a yawning driver, wrapped in a serape and buried under a sombrero, made his appearance, and the mules galloped on their way. There was another long wait at the station, and when the train finally came along we found that the section on the Pullman which we had bought and paid for two days before had been sold again. Fortunately the sleeper was not crowded, so we had no difficulty in obtaining other quarters. I merely mention the fact as an example of Mexican business methods

We were awakened at daybreak to eat a most unsatisfactory breakfast at Acambaro, whence we proceeded sleepily on our way toward Morelia. As usual in Mexico the chilly night was succeeded by a broiling day, and all the charms of the scenery could not allay our discomfort. Nevertheless there are many things on the route between Acambaro and Morelia to interest the tourist. Lake Cuitseo, with its green shade trees, and the mountainous islands rising from its shining breast, is forty miles long and ten miles wide. Its banks are the home of

THE AQUEDUCT, MORELIA.

innumerable water fowl, and its rocky islands are inhabited by fishermen who live in a little world of their own and subsist upon the fish caught in the lake. The shores are, for the most part, salt marshes, from whose sedges rises the smoke of numerous hot springs. Around the famous springs at the foot of the lake are erected crosses, marks of gratitude from the sufferers who have found healing in the waters. For some distance before reaching Morelia the track runs beside a tree-bordered stream. In the shade, waiting for their newly washed clothing to dry, sat men, women and children as naked as bronze statues.

Morelia is another beautiful Mexican city, clean, shining, and with few beggars. We were housed in the Hotel Osguerra, a mansion which was built, to the displeasure of the Morelians, by an extravagant bishop for a private residence. Like many other mansions, it became such a burden to the purse and the conscience of the ecclesiastic that he was only too glad to turn it into a hospital, and give it to the church, and later, with a thrifty desire for a paying investment of the ecclesiastical funds, the holy possessor turned the building into a hotel. Opposite the balcony of the stately rooms assigned to us was the flower-mantled zocalo, and above its riotous luxuriance of vegetation rose the stately domes of the Cathedral. In the center of the zocalo is a monument to the memory of those heroes who have aided Mexico in her struggle for freedom. As for the Cathedral it is the old story—scaffolding, lime-dust, decorators, vandals.

The Calzada of Guadalupe, the favorite promenade of Morelia, is in its way as perfect as the Champs Elysées. Along the sides of the stone-paved avenue extend stone benches and balustrades, and above the heads of the crowds who flock thither day and night, arch the branches of the giant trees. The beautiful Calzada is crossed

THE CALZADA, MORELIA.

in one place by the equally beautiful aqueduct, which strides along on its slender legs, for some distance beside the avenue. The promenade ends in a cluster of pretty parks, one of which, Aztec Park, is a very curious specimen of the tree-trimmer's art.

The sheared evergreens are cut in exact copy of the different Aztec gods, a style of ornamentation which speaks better for the sharpness of the pruning-knife than for the taste of the pruner.

In one of the larger parks the band plays in the evening, and pretty bright-eyed women and gallant young Morelians flock to hear the music—which, I grieve to say, is distinctly bad. On the outside of the ring, on rough benches, sit the peons, regarding the scene with that air of dignified interest so different from the enthusiastic vivacity of the Cuban. The population of Morelia is, however, notwithstanding its seeming gravity, little given to anxious foresight, and it seems not at all to fear the prowling microbe. I was intensely interested one evening in watching the proceedings of a woman who was selling a high-colored, popular drink. A decent-looking Mexican of the middle-class bought a glass of the mixture. The woman added water and sugar to the liquor, stirred the whole with a brass spoon, tasted it, putting the spoon far back in her mouth, added more sugar, tasted it again, and with a final stir handed glass and spoon to the unconcerned purchaser, who swallowed the drink without blenching.

There is a beautiful drive beyond the group of parks, which, as neither horse nor carriage is obtainable in Morelia, seems to be a waste of money and energy. In the neighborhood of the concert park are the ruins of a romantic old chapel.

The main plaza, which is also near the Cathedral, is called the Plaza of the Martyrs, in commemoration of a company of patriots who, in 1830, were executed upon the spot. Here also died, in the year 1814, by the decree of Iturbide, the patriot Matamoras. Indeed, Morelia is famous as the birthplace and the deathplace of heroes. The town, which was formerly called Valladolid, changed its name in honor of one of the best-loved of all the sons of Mexico—Morelos, the last man in the country to die by the Inquisition. The house where this brave man was born is designated by a plaque upon the wall. Within are shown portraits of the patriot and the handkerchief bound around his head when he was shot. Not far from the Cathedral is the old home of Iturbide, the first Emperor of Mexico, who, although a fearless defender of his country's rights, was shot for assuming imperial honors. Doubtless he thought, and with reason, that one who had suffered and sacrificed so much for Mexico was better fitted to be her ruler than a far-away Spanish prince. Unfortunately even the best of patriots are seldom Washingtons.

Morelia glories in the fact that she has the oldest college in Mexico. In the city is also the penitentiary of the State of Michoacan, of which Morelia is

PLAZA DE ARMAS AND CATHEDRAL, GUADALAJARA—*page 259.*

the capital, modeled after that of our own Pennsylvania. To a person who, after a long course of Mexican diet, still retains an appetite, the dulces of the town will appeal strongly, and perhaps there is no reason why they should appeal in vain. I am glad to add that, although Morelia has suffered much in the revolutions, she is now prosperous, and her inhabitants have the air of being well-fed and contented. On the whole Morelia seems to have the cleanest streets, the handsomest and most courteous people, the finest climate and the sweetest air in Mexico.

CHAPTER XXV.

The road from Morelia westward carries the traveler through the lake country of Mexico—a most picturesque region. About ten miles from Morelia are the famous hot springs of Cuincho, said to be a sovereign remedy for rheumatism; but there is no hotel at the place, and there are no bathing facilities. When one remembers the numerous hostelries that surround our springs and the volumes of "analyses" that are distributed around the country, one may well doubt if the Mexicans are really akin to us.

As we crossed the ranges of barren hills that lie an hour's distance from Morelia, we saw one of the native houses wrapped in flames. The owner and his neighbors were gathered around the blazing mass, wringing their hands and crying piteously. Doubtless the result of a whole life's work was represented in the simple household necessaries that were feeding the fire, but even in the "lake country" there was no water, and nothing could be done.

One of the dreams of our Mexican jaunt had been the trip to Tzintzuntzan to see Titian's great picture of the Entombment. Whenever our discomforts seemed too unbearable we consoled each other with the reminder, "In six weeks—in a month—in ten days, we shall see the Titian." So when we reached the station of Patzcuaro and saw the beautiful lake on the hither shore of which lay the promised vision, our exultation was great; but it was destined to be of short duration. We had intended to make Patzcuaro our stopping place, but a glance at the bowlder-strewn road which we must travel three miles in a worm-eaten carriage and in company with a dozen flea-bitten passengers to reach the city sufficed us. We concluded to postpone our visit to Patzcuaro, and to sit instead on the wide verandas of the hacienda on the shore of the lake and contemplate the scene.

Lake Patzcuaro, dropped down among the bold mountains and dotted with rocky islands, is larger than the Swiss Lake Geneva, and is the highest body of navigable water on the Continent. The tall peaks of the islets were reflected in the shining mirror, there was a blue haze over all the picture, and not a puff of air disturbed the living canvas. The blue reaches of water, sizzling in the rays of an

August-like sun, blinded and sickened me; and when I learned that, in order to reach Tzintzuntzan we should be obliged to spend the night at the hacienda, rise at four in the morning and sit all day flat in the boat at the feet of the dirty Indians who would paddle us across the lake, I thought of the

HACIENDA AT LAKE PATZCUARO.

hours of starvation—for we had found the provender furnished by the hacienda impossible stuff— I looked at the lake swimming in the blue heat, and my decision was made. I assured Ahasuerus that if we attempted to cross that lake there would be three entombments instead of one, that I never myself approved of Titian's personal character, that I had seen scores of Titians, and that I didn't believe the picture was a Titian anyway, and in short that

I wasn't going a step. To my surprise Ahasuerus took my decision with edifying meekness and we hied us hungrily away. And that is the true story of our trip to Tzintzuntzan to see the Titian. If we had been in the first flush of triumphant arrival in Mexico we should doubtless have been more persevering, especially as we might have gone around the lake on horseback. Still a thirty-mile ride under the combined disadvantages of a Mexican saddle and a Mexican sun would have been, even to an enthusiast, a trying experience.

The guide-books all agree that Patzcuaro is a very curious old town, and so it is, and so are most Mexican towns. Patzcuaro does certainly possess the advantage of fresh fish two days in the week, but let not the famished wayfarer be too jubilant over that, for the "fish days" will surely come when he is not there. For the rest there is the usual assortment of smells and saints, booths and beggars, market women and mountebanks. The word Patzcuaro signifies "place of delights," but I think the ordinary traveler will take the "delights" soberly and without in the least losing his head. At all events, the familiar towers of Morelia looked very charming to us as we skirted the stream and rolled again into the pretty station.

We left Morelia one morning by the freight train, that we might be sure of making connections with the northbound express at Acambaro, as a breakfast we had encountered a few days before in that city did not incline our hearts to stay over night there. Now Ahasuerus and I never did a particularly shrewd thing without fatal results, and on this occasion our usual fortune lay in wait for us. We had a hot box; we were shunted on to a side track, where we lay for hours; we sat all day in a hot, stuffy caboose; and we had the satisfaction of seeing the distrusted passenger train rush past us on its way to make the desired connection, which it did for the first time in three months. However, we did not propose to be cast down by trifles, so we turned to exasperating fortune a smiling face, and insincerely congratulated ourselves upon the admirable opportunity given us to see Acambaro. In support of this position we ambled aimlessly up and down in the deep sand, and then came wearily back, and ate an unwashen supper with unwashen hands, while the household, with many maneuvers and much bustle, prepared our room for the night. The room at last assigned us was Number 9. Besides ourselves it had various other claimants. It belonged to a conductor who "run on Number Four," and an engineer who "run on Eleven," besides a train dispatcher and a Mexican commercial traveler who openly and violently accused us of stealing his "grip." These several claimants, at intervals during the night, made their claims known by kicks and blows upon our portal, and by loud and emphatic cries of "Open the door," "Come out of that, won't you?" "What are you doing with my grip?" and other embarrassing remarks. We might have thought ourselves in the house of a tailor, and that every one of him had come home late.

These individuals had hardly ceased the recital of their wrongs when it was time to get up and catch the morning train, so we stumbled sleepily down to our rolls and coffee. I never think now of those early risings without a bone-aching, swimming sensation. If the time ever comes when Mexico is sufficiently civilized to introduce night trains, the lot of the traveler will certainly be less woeful.

CHAPTER XXVI.

The combination of dirt and dulces in Celaya is altogether too overpowering for an American stomach. "Dulces?" I exclaimed to a persistent vender of the dainties. "Dulces in all this filth!" I spoke in English that I might spare his sensitive feelings, but I soon found the precaution useless, for neither dulce merchant nor opal peddler possessed tender sensibilities. In spite of our most discouraging looks, the women and children on the pavement, the street-car conductors, the hotel clerks, bell-boys and waiters, in turn pulled from their pockets the familiar little packages of black paper, containing watery, lifeless opals, which they displayed to our wearied eyes, exclaiming *"Bonita, senor; Muy hermosa, senora!"* Sometimes these pertinacious venders baited their hook by addressing me as "beautiful señorita"—an impolitic course of conduct which still further hardened my already flinty heart against them.

Celaya is said to be a very interesting town, but

the atmosphere of the place did not harmonize with our mood, so we concluded to go on to Irapuato for the night. Here we found a frank-faced young American who took us to his little hotel, furnished with clean beds, snowy towels, and blessed hot water. We were in the seventh heaven and went to bed early that we might make the most of the delightful American springs and mattresses; but our hopes of a refreshing sleep were soon dissipated, for a Mexican family next door proceeded to make the night hideous with their revels. In vain the guests appeared at their respective windows with pitiful protests, in vain the landlord argued and threatened. At four o'clock he was obliged to send for the police to compel order, and then it was time to get up for the morning train.

We were blear-eyed and dizzy from sleeplessness when we boarded the Guadalajara train, and continued on our weary round of pleasure. We were soon speeding through unpicturesque but fertile regions. The country west of Irapuato might, from outward seeming, be Illinois or Iowa, but the barns of the Mexican farmer are unique. They have roots, they increase in size from year to year, and they attend to their own repairs. In short, the trees are the barns, upon whose branches the two corn harvests of the year are stored during the long and rainless winters. This is one of the richest agricultural regions in Mexico, and the haciendas look more modern than in other parts of the country. At the station of Atequiza, a short distance this side of Guadalajara, is an immense hacienda which has its own railway and electric lights.

We had promised ourselves a delightful season in Guadalajara, which is said to be the prettiest and most modern town in Mexico. If we were somewhat disappointed I must lay it to the heat and the dust, and not to any lack in Guadalajara. The season was late for pleasure-seekers, and we were the last of the winter tourists. I can imagine that when the rains come and wash off the dust-buried roses, hibiscus and orange trees, and when the thousands of blooming plants in the plaza cast their fragrance on the soft air, that Guadalajara is a paradise. It certainly possesses one of the promised blessings of paradise—the houris—for the women of the town are, with few exceptions, beautiful. The proportion of white faces is larger than in the other Mexican cities, and if these dark-eyed daughters of the south possessed a queenly carriage they would be peerless; but, unfortunately for the doctrines of the Dress-Reform League, these women, the daughters of mothers who wore the rebosa, the chemise and the sandal, are entirely lacking in that grace and symmetry of form so natural to the whale-boned daughters of our own land. I fear we cannot give to

Greek raiment the entire credit for the wonderful perfection of the ancient Greek form.

The public buildings of Guadalajara are really fine. Over the doorway of one of the municipal palaces is this reminder, "Except the Lord keepeth the city, the watchman waketh in vain." Such an audacious mixture of politics and religion would surely be tolerated only in a half-civilized community. In the Cathedral of Guadalajara is one of the treasures of Mexico—an Assumption of the Virgin, by Murillo. The face of the Virgin is the same face of white innocence—a little older—that we know so well in the Immaculate Conception. The difficulty in seeing the picture amounts almost to a prohibition, and the Mexican government should take steps to make the public sharers in the delights of this great painting. We made repeated unsuccessful attempts to see the treasure, but our determined perseverance at lâst won the day. Upon our first visit we were received by the doorkeeper of the Cathedral, who accepted a generous fee, and then handed us on to the sacristan—who also received a fee—and who ushered us into a dark, dirty closet where he left us with the request to "Wait a minute." We waited many minutes; then an acolyte came by, who to our request to see the picture answered, "Wait a minute." Then a priest passed through the room who deigned to listen to our prayer and who conjured us to "Wait a minute." Then the faithless sacristan again appeared and said, "Wait just a little minute, señor," and seemingly disappeared off from the face of the earth. But the chill of the stone bench upon which we sat, combined with our fiery, untamed American natures, moved us at this point to come away, grumbling at having wasted the whole forenoon in "waiting a minute." A few days after, however, we met in the Cathedral a party of the higher clergy who not only listened to our prayer, but courteously escorted us to the sacristy where the picture hung, and gave us permission to seat ourselves and study it at leisure.

The markets of Guadalajara are the finest in Mexico. There is no suspicion of filth or decay in the bright fresh fruits and fragrant blossoms piled upon the long tables. The products of all climes are at the very door of Guadalajara, for although the town itself is in a temperate region, a descent of 3,000 feet into the Barranca brings the traveler into the tropics. This is a hard trip, and an exciting one, down a narrow mountain trail where the pensive little donkeys, stopping to meditate, choose the most hair-raising precipices for their reflections. In the bottom of the Barranca runs the Lerma River, which is crossed by an absurd little ferry.

There is, not far from the plaza, an Hospicio, much

applauded by the guide-books, which is supported by the government for the ostensible purpose of teaching useful arts to orphan boys and girls. As we were specially interested in this line of work, Ahasuerus took some trouble to obtain permits to visit the institution. When we arrived at the Hospicio we were given an application for rheumatism in the shape of seats on a cold, stone bench in an icy hall, where we waited an hour for the coming of the Sister who was to show us through the building. When she did at last appear she seemed to be under the vow of perpetual silence. She galloped us through a long hall to a refectory door which she deigned to open an inch, gave us a peep into a dormitory window, hustled us through a gaudy, tasteless chapel, and back again to the door. Evidently the Hospicio does not approve of curious strangers who might ask questions. We saw few children, and those few were spiritless little souls, and there was no childish noise about the building. We could not help contrasting our reception and the seeming desolation of the place with the hospitable air, and active, cheerful life of the government training school at Guadalupe near Zacetecas.

During the first few days of our stay in Guadalajara we went every evening to hear the band play in the beautiful plaza. The music was very good, and was enjoyed by an appreciative and enthusiastic audience. The concert generally ended with "Cuba Libre," whose strains elicited from the impulsive and liberty-loving Mexicans storms of applause. But one morning, when we went upon the street, we noticed an excitement among the people. Messengers with the left arm bound in crape were hurrying around distributing huge black-bordered envelopes. These, as we afterward learned, contained tidings of the sudden death of the general commanding the State of Guadalajara. There were no more park concerts, and the city seemed restless and gloomy, Changes in the government are feared no less in Mexico than in France.

One of the suburbs of Guadalajara is San Pedro, where live the famous potters who make the finest Mexican ware. The Mexican pottery is exceedingly fragile, and the utmost care is necessary in packing it for transportation. The few pieces in which I invested were soon nothing but glittering dust. The Indian sculptors whose work attracted so much attention at the Chicago Exposition have their workshop in San Pedro. They make little busts and statuettes, and for a small sum the traveler can, in a few hours, have a very satisfactory bust of himself or of his photographed friends.

To reach the famous Falls of San Juanacatlan we went by rail to the little station of El Castillo, a distance of twelve or fifteen miles from Guadalajara. Thence we took a mule-car to the Falls. We had, on this expedition our usual escort of leather-jacketed soldiers, for no train or tram-car leaves any station in Mexico without this armed guard. Personally I liked these toy warriors and felt very safe

FALLS OF SAN JUANACATLAN

in the shadow of their sombreros, but Ahasuerus openly scoffed at them, and declared that they turned their toes in when they marched. Indeed, that zealous martinet evinced an inordinate desire to drill the entire Mexican army.

Under the protection of these pigeon-toed guardians of the republic we arrived safely at the Falls. San Juanacatlan bears a striking resemblance in miniature to Niagara. The Fall, which is about seventy-five feet high, must be a mine of wealth to the owner of the hacienda; for it furnishes the power for lighting Guadalajara, and it will in future be pressed into service by a fine mill, as yet uncompleted, which is to be fitted with all the modern improvements in machinery.

Our traveling companions on this trip were an interesting company. There was a bright-faced young Frenchman, a low-browed, unprepossessing Spaniard, a German commercial traveler, two courtly and affable Mexicans, a coffee-planter from the Isthmus of Tehuantepec who claimed citizenship in Kansas, and ourselves. There were all the materials for a successful composite photograph.

The beautiful Lake Chapala, which lies in the foot-hills not far from Guadalajara, is the summer residence of the wealthy city people. Lake Chapala, which is one hundred miles long and twenty-five wide, is the largest lake in Mexico. The verdant rim of this charming basin of water is surrounded by handsome homes, and the hot springs along its shores furnish delightful and health-giving baths. Before we left Guadalajara summer was coming on apace, and the morning trains to Cha-

UP TAIASOPA CAÑON BETWEEN THE TUNNELS—*page 269.*

pala were crowded with family parties—with pretty, modest maidens, short-jacketed youths, hunters, dogs and pleasure-seekers. It was the same scene we have so often witnessed in our own land, on the continent and in England. The summer-resort instinct seems to be a part of human nature, and it probably descends from as far back as Adam and Eve. I have no doubt that if the fair mother of the race had been allowed to remain in Eden she would have built a row of summer cottages and a summer hotel before the end of the second year.

CHAPTER XXVII.

The traveler should not fail to buy strawberries at Irapuato. They are brought to the train at every season of the year, and are always good, but in April they are in their perfection. They are packed hulls down in large baskets with curiously twisted handles, and the globes of vivid scarlet, seedless, pulp, as big as plums and as sweet as honey, are as tempting to the eye as to the palate. In nearly every state in Mexico just such strawberries might be raised, but for some reason Irapuato furnishes the only crop of the kind.

We had another terrible night at Celaya, another struggle with filth, mosquitoes, dulce peddlers and opal venders, and then we turned our faces northward to San Luis Potosi, passing on the way the pretty city of San Miguel de Allende. This town has fine terraced gardens and a church with a pig-loving saint. The saint has a very dolorous outlook on the world, doubtless because his fine antique pig has been replaced by a hopelessly modern and porkish one. Another member of the canonized fraternity in the Casa Santa has had his bones inserted into a body of wax and endeavors to look as much like a sure-enough, live saint as possible.

San Miguel de Allende takes its name from the patriot and revolutionist Allende, who aided Hidalgo in his struggle for liberty. A short distance from San Miguel is the little town of Atotonilco, with the humble church from whose altar Hidalgo snatched the banner of Our Lady of Guadalupe—the banner which was to become the standard of Mexico. We had promised ourselves the privilege of a reverent pilgrimage to the town of Hidalgo-Dolores—to the home, the church and the beehives of our hero, but the town was infected with smallpox, and therefore unsafe for strangers. From Hidalgo-Dolores the young curé and patriot, issued his grito, or call to arms. To his holy standard flocked many of the neighboring vil-

MEXICAN NAT. R. R. STATION, SAN LUIS POTOSI.

lagers, among them Allende, who brought with him the Queen's Regiment in which he was an officer.

We found San Luis Potosi to be a great mining town, dusty and comfortless, with a sun-burned plaza. It, too, was infected with the smallpox, and we were glad to get out of it. The only impressive thing about our stay in San Luis Potosi was our first dinner, which consisted of five beef courses; beef soup,, boiled beef with chili, a ragout of beef with carrots, roast beef, and a salad of cold beef and potatoes. I was reminded that I used in my school days to read in the Physical Geography, "Man, in the tropics, lives principally on vegetable food."

As we strolled one day through the town we met a party of excursionists who greeted us warmly and inquired, "What party are you with?" When we explained that we were our own party, they cried aghast, "What, down here all alone!" Upon our further explanation that we had not been alone at all, but that in fact we had sometimes had only too much company, they regarded us with commiseration, demanding as a final clincher, "But what have you had to eat?" It was impossible to convince these doubting souls that we quite often had a very fair meal, and that the French restaurants in the City of Mexico were as good as the ordinary restaurants in Paris. They evidently considered us very eccentric, and returned to their Pullman cars with an amusing assumption of superiority.

From San Luis Potosi we took the Mexican Central R. R. to Tampico, not because we wished to see Tampico, which is jungle-like and malarious to a degree, but because we wished to see the most wonderful bit of scenery in Mexico, the Tamasopa Cañon. As a sight-seeing expedition our trip was a failure, but as a stimulus to imagination it was eminently successful. Just before we reached Canoas, where the descent into the cañon begins, a heavy fog enveloped us. But the regular trains do not wait upon the weather, so we slipped by the long excursion train of our San Luis Potosi acquaintances, which was waiting for the weather to clear, and rolled over the edge of the precipice. It was a fairy-like experience. Sometimes we seemed to be adrift in fleecy vapors, sometimes to be running along the edge of the sky, looking down upon a shadowy world below. The white mist curled around us like feathers; giant branches of orchid-decked trees flashed out of the curtain and were gone again, and filmy masses of tropical vegetation swung like cobwebs in the silver ether. Certainly the ride down the cañon on a clear day can not be so magically beautiful as it was in the fog. The clouds lifted as we reached the foot of the descent and we found everything in the valley dripping with moisture. The station of Rascon—according to railroad men the unhealthiest spot in Mexico—is situated in a moldy jungle. The company intended to move their buildings to some place where the sanitary conditions are better, and perhaps they have done so before now. With the railroad station will probably go the few squalid huts which form the so-called town.

The accommodating fog lifted again long enough for us to see the wonderful string of cascades—El Salto del Abra—which are of the most exquisite tint of robin's egg blue. This chain of waterfalls is more than a mile long, and one of the falls is three hundred feet high. Somewhere down there, where the river tumbles and foams, is Choy's Cave; but as the regular trains do not stop for caves we were compelled to go mournfully on our way.

The last grade—the Cañon of El Salto del Abra—took us down to the plains. At Las Palmas, at the foot of the descent, the trains from both directions were huddled, awaiting orders. The fog had interfered with the time table, and both engines and engineers looked sullen. We strolled around the little Chinese eating-house, taking notes of railroad complications and vexations. "Number Four" was lost. As the other engines came panting up to the station, the engineers rushed into the office to receive their orders, and were met by an account of

"Number Four's" delinquencies. I do not know how "Number Four," when she finally came in, explained her conduct, but she did come in safely at last, closely followed by the excursion train which we had left at Canoas, waiting for the weather to clear up. The excursionists had seen nothing at all of the wonders we had seen, and were damp, cross and disgusted.

For some time after the arrival of the tardy trains Las Palmas was a scene of confusion, and I wondered what the dead and gone Aztecs, sleeping in their ruined cities not far from us, would say if they could suddenly rise from their graves and hear the babble of strange tongues and the shriek of the monster engines. But one by one the long trains at last pulled out, and went winking off into the night, while the east-bound passengers crossed the plains and the rivers Tamesi and Panuco, and in the darkness rolled into Tampico.

Tampico resembles in some respects the Gulf cities of our own land. It is damp, unhealthy, odorous, but it has the best harbor in Mexico, and doubtless will be, in the near future one of the large cities of the republic. A fine beach about eight miles from the town furnishes delightful sea-bathing. The low shores, upon which Tampico is built, are uninteresting; but the high bluffs which rise further back from the river might, and probably soon will be, utilized for residence purposes.

As we journeyed back to San Luis Potosi we chatted with our fellow-passengers—American railroad officials and employes, with their wives. After the manner of our sex, we women discussed together the subject of housekeeping, particularly the comparative advantages of housekeeping in Mexico and in the United States. I found that they were all homesick, and they gave but a sorry account of the domestic outlook for Americans in Mexico. It is difficult to find schools for the children, as it is dangerous to send a child to the municipal schools where contagious diseases are not quarantined. Then, too, household supplies are poor and high-priced. One cannot exist on drawn-work, silver filagree, leather belts or card cases, and these staples are almost the only cheap thing in Mexico. Fruit in tin cans costs $1.75 a can, bacon from 60 to 80 cents a pound, butter from 80 cents to $1. It is impossible to find shoes for American feet in the country, most of the clothing must come from the United States, and as the tariff is high, dry goods are expensive. In short, a family can live better in the United States on a given salary than it can in Mexico on more than twice the amount. It was the same old story; my countrywomen, like all good Americans in a foreign land, felt themselves to be exiles in the midst of hardships.

CHAPTER XXVIII.

It was very hot the day we left San Luis Potosi and the unreasonable heat showed no sign of abatement, even after we had passed the stone that marks the location of the Tropic of Cancer and knew positively that we were in the Temperate Zone. Catorce, which lies buried in a deep chasm a short distance from the railroad, is one of the most picturesque towns in Mexico, and certainly merits a visit. But when we saw the beds of dust through which we must travel on foot or on horseback to reach that city of mines and abysses, no thrill of enthusiasm stirred our investigating souls, and we retired beneath the curtains of the sleeper, with premonitions of a martyr's fate. It was then with delight that, when we were dragged from our beds in the dead of night, we found the last trace of the torrid zone had disappeared; a north wind was blowing, and a cold rain, which fell like a benediction on our inflamed and sun-dried faces, was dropping steadily.

To reach the battlefield of Buena Vista one must

leave the train at Saltillo, a town about fifty miles from Monterey. The battlefield is six miles from the town, and as Saltillo is as yet without street cars it is necessary to hire a carriage to make the trip. The battle of Buena Vista—or Angostura, as the Mexicans call it—was fought in a deep valley rimmed with mountains. In the midst of the valley rises a high plateau which falls away on both sides into sharp ravines. Upon this plateau General Taylor with an army of 5,000 men took his stand against 12,000 Mexicans, commanded by General Santa Anna. In the hard-fought battle which followed the Americans were victorious, although at a terrible cost of life. Among the killed were Colonel John Hardin and a son of Henry Clay. The Mississippi Rifles, commanded by Colonel Jefferson Davis, did valiant service in this battle. One of Whittier's early poems, "The Angels of Buena Vista," pays a most touching tribute to the Mexican women who ministered to our wounded after the battle.

The great State of Coahuila, of which Saltillo is the capital, once included all of Texas. Although the United States has taken most of her territory, our country has as yet little influenced the capital city, which is thoroughly Mexican in its sentiments and customs. The chief business of the town is the manufacture of the Saltillo serapes, which are said to be the best made in the republic. The leisure hours of the citizens seem to be spent shrugging themselves in the folds of these serapes in the vain effort to warm their frozen bodies by the glow

BISHOP'S PALACE, MONTEREY.

of the blankets' bright colors. In spite of our impressions, however, the climate is said to be delightful in pleasant weather.

When we reached Monterey at four o'clock in the morning, it was cold and rainy, and we unpacked the heavy wraps we had carried so long through the tropics. There was no conveyance at the station but an open street car with water-logged benches. So we were compelled to put ourselves to soak behind its dripping curtains during the long journey to the hotel, where we completed the hydropathic treatment by sleeping some hours between wet sheets. We arose betimes, and, voiceless and disgusted, after a mere pretense of breakfast, we went out to see the town.

Monterey can hardly be called a Mexican city. It has a large and constantly increasing American population, and American ways of doing business. Here, for the first time in Mexico, we saw drawn-work and opals take on American prices, and we found also American prices at the hotel—accompanied by the very poorest kind of Mexican food and service. It will not be long, however, before Monterey, like Chihuahua, will lose the last vestige of its Mexican picturesqueness, and become an ordinary American city. Nevertheless, as its beauty depends in no small measure upon its natural situation, Monterey can never become wholly uninteresting. The great Saddle Mountain which overtops the busy streets is the only saddle mountain I ever saw which did not have to be explained to me; the saddle is actually visible to the naked and uninstructed eye—a fact which of itself should make Monterey notable.

To find any particular place in Monterey just take the Belt Line of mule-cars. Every other line in the city branches off from this, and if you miss connections the first time, you can swing around the circle again. We took three swings before we finally found the trail to the Bishop's Palace, although most of the time the palace was in full view. This palace, which was built by one of Monterey's bishop's for a country home, was besieged and taken by our army during the Mexican war, and its capture gave the city into the hands of the Americans. After the fall of the citadel, General Worth, commanding the United States forces, entered the town, but finding its streets swept by the fire of the Mexican artillery, his troops broke through the walls of the houses, in this manner making their way from block to block, while the sharpshooters from the roofs poured a ceaseless shower of bullets upon the heads of the city's brave defenders. Although I am aware that the officers and soldiers of the United States' army could, under the circumstances, not do otherwise, still, I am never less proud of them than when I read the annals of the Mexican War.

At present a garrison of Mexicans is encamped in the desolated halls of the palace, and the once beautiful gardens are turned to waste land; but at the foot of the hill, where lies Monterey, rimmed round with majestic hills and mountains, are pleasant homes in sunny orchards and the air that rises to us is filled with the odor of orange blossoms. Surely war never turned into desolation a more beautiful spot.

A little river which has for its source the Oja Agua, runs through Monterey. It is crossed by a famous old bridge, La Purisima, the scene of one of the desperate stands made by the Mexicans against our troops. The Topo Chico Hot Springs, which can be reached by horse cars, are about four miles from the city. The drive to the springs through fields of waving grain—which in April are ripe for the harvest—is charming. The springs are said to be sovereign for rheumatism and kindred diseases. Whether or not they are curative, they certainly are cleansing and delightful. The water, which has a temperature of one hundred and six degrees, is soft as velvet and of a most beautiful blue color; the tubs are clean and although the great bath halls are cold and cheerless in winter, they must be refreshingly cool in summer. Near the bathhouse are two fairly comfortable hotels. One of them—built of black marble—makes some effort, I believe, to furnish modern accommodations.

280   MEXICAN VISTAS

The windows of our room at the hotel looked out upon the little Hidalgo Park, in the center of which is a monument bearing a figure of the great patriot in whose honor it was named. The little plaza is

HIDALGO PARK, MONTEREY.

clean, and bright with flowers, a living contrast to the dead pile of awkward modern buildings, not far distant, which Monterey calls her Cathedral. Hidalgo among the flowers seems a type of life ever upspringing in comparison to the dead pile of stones, and his uplifted hand seems to challenge the

verdict of that outlived church which excommunicated him and agreed to his death. As we all
know, however, the conscience of the Mexican
church has been its own challenger, and the remains
of this, one of the greatest, if one of the most rebel-
lious, of her sons, rests in her holiest place. The
great plaza or Alameda at the other end of Monterey is a curious combination of American thrift
and the Mexican love for the picturesque. The
plazas, as well as many of the streets and public
buildings, were, at the time of our visit to Monterey,
gay with bunting and floral decorations, as it was
the anniversary of the retaking of Puebla from the
French by President Diaz.

CHAPTER XXIX.

We left Montercy one evening when the city was celebrating with the blare of trumpets and the flare of fireworks, her martial anniversary, and turned our faces homeward. All the next day we rolled through gorgeous gardens of orange, gold and scarlet cactus, and through fields of wavy mesquite, but we would have given all that tropic wealth of color and bloom for the blossom of our own dandelion. We had had smiles and tears together, but for the moment we were only too glad to say goodbye to old Mexico, and greet again our own land; that land we had left in peace, and which was now filled with the sound of marching troops and the trappings of war. Like loyal Americans everywhere, we were anxious to be at home and bear our part in the great drama.

It is much easier—and cheaper—to get in to Mexico than it is to get out of it. The little money that I had left in my purse was suddenly divided by two, and as an addition to my pecuniary distress the

Custom House officers, who on this side have a vigilant eye for smugglers, inquired the first thing if I had any drawn-work. Now why did they ask me that? Other women on the train brought through all sorts of contraband goods without any troublesome questions. Was it because I alone looked guilty? I am sure I did not feel so, for I had known of hundreds of dollars' worth of drawn-work passing the border without challenge, and consequently I never thought of paying duty for my modest store. But the ways of the Custom House are past finding out. I have known women to smuggle with the greatest audacity, and without one word of suspicion, while the most pious and conscientious woman I ever knew was once accused of fraud, and with difficulty rescued her sealskin coat—which she had carried abroad with her the year before—from the clutches of the customs officers. I suppose, however, that the officials must collect tariff from somebody, and perhaps they were as lenient with me as the law allows; at all events they did not make me pay any duty on my dear old Aztec gods, so I will forgive them.

In spite of the Custom House we were radiantly happy when we had crossed the border and were really once more in the United States. We made our obeisances to the first derby hat we met, and the sight of the good American clothes, that looked as if they would stay on, thrilled us with joy. To be sure our ardor was a little dampened by the appearance of a particularly grumpy Pullman-car conductor, and when we reflected that we had never seen a discourteous act or heard a discourteous word from any railway or street-car employe in Mexico, our patriotic pride was a little staggered; but fortunately we remembered, just in time to save our feelings, that the American, in spite of his un-Chesterfieldian ways, doubtless possessed manly qualities unknown to the polite Mexican. He certainly had the ruder, and, let us hope, the stronger, virtues.

And the wooden shanties along the road—how delightfully clean and fresh their unpainted walls looked to us! Who is it that says our wooden cabins are undignified, inartistic? To be sure they are cold in winter and warm in summer, but the fresh air blows through them and the hot sun sizzles out their germs and there is no incrusting filth of generations on their walls. Then how easily they burn up when their day of usefulness is over; and even if they do burn up their inmates, that at least is a clean death and far better than poison by typhus. Yes, I love even the wooden shanties of my own country, and, in spite of mental reservations on the subject of the Mexican war, I am so proud to have been born in the United States, that, if I could fight for the dear old land with baking powder instead of gunpowder, I would be one of her most valiant defenders.

www.ingramcontent.com/pod-product-compliance
Lightning Source LLC
Chambersburg PA
CBHW022053230426
43672CB00008B/1157